GOVERNANCE OF INTERNATIONAL STRATEGIC ALLIANCES

GOVERNANCE OF INTERNATIONAL STRATEGIC ALLIANCES
Technology and Transaction Costs

JOANNE E. OXLEY

Volume 28

Routledge
Taylor & Francis Group

LONDON AND NEW YORK

First published in 1999

This edition first published in 2013
by Routledge
2 Park Square, Milton Park, Abingdon, Oxon, OX14 4RN

Simultaneously published in the USA and Canada
by Routledge
711 Third Avenue, New York, NY 10017

Routledge is an imprint of the Taylor & Francis Group, an informa business

British Library Cataloguing in Publication Data
A catalogue record for this book is available from the British Library

ISBN: 978-0-415-63009-2 (Set)
eISBN: 978-0-203-07716-0 (Set)
ISBN: 978-0-415-65768-6 (Volume 28)
eISBN: 978-0-203-07662-0 (Volume 28)

Publisher's Note
The publisher has gone to great lengths to ensure the quality of this reprint but
points out that some imperfections in the original copies may be apparent.

Disclaimer
The publisher has made every effort to trace copyright holders and would
welcome correspondence from those they have been unable to trace.

Printed and bound by CPI Group (UK) Ltd, Croydon, CR0 4YY

Governance of International Strategic Alliances

Technology and Transaction Costs

Joanne E. Oxley

University of Michigan Business School
Ann Arbor, Michigan, USA

harwood academic publishers

Australia • Canada • China • France • Germany • India •
Japan • Luxembourg • Malaysia • The Netherlands •
Russia • Singapore • Switzerland

Amsteldijk 166
1st Floor
1079 LH Amsterdam
The Netherlands

British Library Cataloguing in Publication Data

Oxley, Joanne E.
    Governance of international strategic alliances :
    technology and transaction costs. – (Studies in global
    competition ; v. 7 – ISSN 1023-6147)
    1. Strategic alliances (Business) – Management
    2. International economic relations   3. Transaction costs
    I. Title
    658.4'012

ISBN   90-5702-591-4

To *John* and *Alana*

CONTENTS

FIGURES

TABLES

ACKNOWLEDGMENTS

This book and the dissertation on which it is based would not have been possible without the assistance and support of many people. I am most fortunate to have counted among my teachers many outstanding faculty at the University of California, Berkeley, from early models and mentors such as Janet Yellen and David Vogel, to my dissertation committee: Oliver Williamson, David Mowery and Bronwyn Hall. I am deeply indebted to each of them for their generosity and wisdom. I also thank all my fellow students at Berkeley, most especially Chris Ahmadjian, Janet Bercovitz, Karen Schnietz, Brian Silverman and Emerson Tiller, for their many contributions to my work.

In developing the ideas expressed in this book, I have benefited greatly from the comments of seminar participants at several universities and conferences, and from colleagues at the University of Michigan, particularly Francine LaFontaine, Scott Masten and Bernard Yeung. I thank them all for their insight.

Financial support for the research was gratefully received from the Orel Crawford Foundation, Bradley Foundation, and John M. Olin Foundation.

Finally, I would like to thank the many friends and family members who provided the moral and emotional support I needed to complete this project with (I hope) my sanity and humor intact.

ONE

Introduction

Why do firms establish strategic alliances? How should they organize an alliance for maximum effectiveness? What difference does it make (if any) when the firms in an alliance are headquartered in different nations? As the rate at which firms established international strategic alliances exploded in the early 1980s (see figure 1.1), researchers became intrigued by these and related questions and a large, disparate literature on the subject of inter-firm alliances developed. In the process, consensus has emerged regarding some aspects of alliance activity. For example, there is general acceptance that the growth and internationalization of alliances stems from a confluence of trends in the global economy. These include the increased pace of technological development and the need to combine disparate areas of technical expertise, as technological fields converge, (Mowery, 1989) and the sources of "leading edge" technologies become geographically dispersed (Hladik, 1985; Scherer, 1992).

When it comes to the structuring and management of alliances, however, significant controversy remains. There is a plethora of practitioner-oriented volumes offering advice on alliance management, but each work reflects the idiosyncratic experience and viewpoint of the author, and generalizable conclusions are difficult to identify. Among theoreticians, there is a similar lack of agreement: some authors emphasize the role of organizational learning within alliances, and so focus on organizational design or management processes to support information exchange (e.g., Inkpen, 1996). Others argue that "trust" between alliance partners is of central concern, and these authors explore the establishment of norms of reciprocity within alliances (Gulati, 1995a, 1995b). Still others see alliances as a means to coordinate market actions in oligopolistic markets,

1

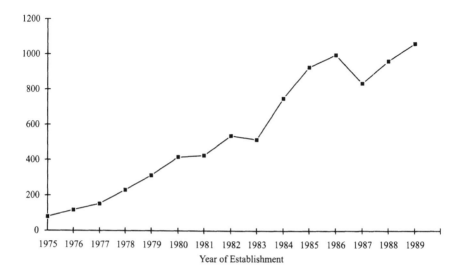

Figure 1.1   Strategic Alliance Formation, 1975–89
Source: CATI database

with potentially anticompetitive effects (Porter & Fuller, 1986), or as governance structures for enhancing the efficiency of inter-firm exchange (Dyer & Singh, in press; Pisano, Russo, & Teece, 1988).

The variety of perspectives brought to bear on the study of inter-firm alliances has been largely constructive, increasing the range of questions addressed and broadening our understanding of this important aspect of firm behavior in the global economy. In some cases, however, progress has been hampered by a lack of dialogue between researchers in different fields. The study described here aims to stimulate discussion by articulating a systematic approach to the analysis of one particular aspect of inter-firm alliance behavior, i.e. the choice of organizational form in both domestic and international strategic alliances. This is an important issue, since variety in alliance types has grown over the past decades, almost as rapidly as the overall rate of alliance formation itself. In addition to the equity joint venture — the "traditional" alliance form — inter-firm linkages now run the gamut from fairly simple technology licensing agreements to joint marketing agreements, research corporations and consortia, and "strategic" customer-supplier partnerships (see figure 1.2). Developing the logic by which firms can choose among these various alliance forms is an important element in the overall understanding of inter-firm alliances, and provides a structured framework for looking at more "micro" aspects of alliance management.

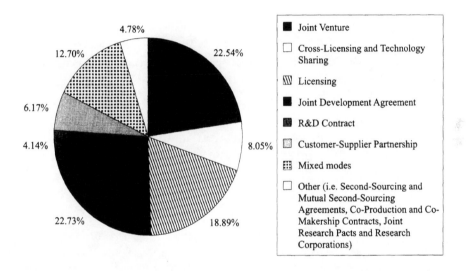

Figure 1.2 Organizational Forms of Technology Alliances in the '80s
Source: CATI Database

The theoretical perspective adopted in the study is transaction cost economics (TCE), an approach centrally concerned with decisions regarding the efficient boundaries of the firm (Williamson, 1985). In this paradigm, organizations are characterized as governance structures, lying on a continuum from classical markets (i.e. arms-length contracts) to hierarchy (internal organization). Strategic alliances and other intermediate governance forms, (so-called "hybrids") lie between these two polar forms. A key argument in transaction cost economics is that transactions are assigned to governance structures so as to effect a discriminating — mainly transaction cost economizing — match (Williamson, 1991). This implies that choosing the appropriate organizational form for an inter-firm alliance requires examination of the characteristics of planned activities (the transaction) to assess potential "hazards" associated with a reliance on simple contracts. Attributes of the organizational alternatives available are examined, and their relative efficacy in mitigating the identified contracting hazards weighed, to identify the most efficient "match."

Governance of international strategic alliances is, of course, not a new area of research: there is a well-established literature focusing on the multinational corporation that has been extended in recent years to encompass international joint ventures and strategic alliances. However, the development of this literature has proceeded in apparent isolation from mainstream organization theory. An implicit assumption in international management research has often been that questions of *international* organization are "different in kind" and cannot be handled by a more parsimonious logic of organization. In order to confront this issue here, a transaction cost economics model of international business arrangements is developed, showing that the apparently idiosyncratic features of international organization are informed by the same logic that has been extensively documented in the domestic context.

Although there have been previous attempts to provide useful taxonomies of the large variety of inter-firm alliances (e.g., Contractor & Lorange, 1988; Lorange & Roos, 1992) a need remains for a model of inter-firm alliances that is tightly connected to underlying theoretical constructs. A contribution of this study is to more thoroughly describe a "market-hierarchy continuum" of hybrid forms, based on a comparative analysis of the governance features of different types of agreement. The focus is on mechanisms such as monitoring devices, hostage exchanges and dispute settlement procedures that serve to attenuate contracting hazards in international strategic alliances.

As suggested above, the challenges of technology development and transfer account for much of the popularity of strategic alliances in recent decades. Study of these alliances provides an opportunity to examine a form of contractual hazards that previously has been underdeveloped in transaction cost economics — i.e. hazards related to weak property rights — since firms establishing strategic alliances must beware the potential for leakage of valuable intellectual property (Teece, 1986). Although these so-called "appropriability hazards" are a well-accepted characteristic of technology contracts (Levin, Klevorick, Nelson, & Winter, 1987) there has been little systematic examination of how appropriability hazards can be mitigated within different types of inter-firm alliance. I suggest that this is in part due to a failure to sufficiently disaggregate the factors that affect the level of appropriability hazards inherent to a particular transaction. Review and synthesis of the literatures on the economics of information, intellectual property protection, and governance, lead to the identification of three aspects of the "appropriability problem": (i) specification of intellectual property rights; (ii) monitoring; and (iii) enforcement.

This formulation of the appropriability problem forms the basis of an empirical analysis of appropriability hazards and governance mode choice, first in "domestic" strategic alliances (involving only US-based firms) and subsequently in international alliances. Consistent with transaction cost logic, results of this analysis suggest that more "hierarchical" alliances are chosen for transactions where contracting hazards are more severe: for samples of alliances drawn from the Cooperative Agreements and Technology Indicators (CATI) database, I show that more complex contracts or equity joint ventures are chosen when property rights associated with the technology are difficult to specify in a contract and when the scope of activities is wider, so that monitoring of activities is hampered. Furthermore, in US firms' international alliances, the strength of intellectual property protection in the "foreign" country has a significant impact on the choice of organizational form.

The close correspondence between empirical results from analysis of samples of domestic alliances and international alliances provides compelling support for the contention that international strategic alliances are informed by the same logic as alliances in the domestic context. Firms operating in the international arena need not "throw away" the lessons learned in their domestic operations, but must pay close attention to details of the institutional environment in the countries in which they do business, and fold these into the analysis. Furthermore, the significance of intellectual property regimes in explaining variance in international alliance forms highlights the importance of firms' concerns about technology leakage in strategic alliances.

The analysis also informs another area of controversy in the literature, i.e., the apparent dichotomy between the need to mitigate hazards associated with opportunistic behavior by alliance partners and the desire to "learn" from those same alliance partners. I suggest (and provide supportive empirical results) that this dichotomy, between learning and hazard mitigation in alliances, is in fact a *false* dichotomy. Critics of the transaction cost approach to analysis of alliances overlook the role of "credible commitments" in enhancing learning opportunities, through the lowering of incentives to engage in opportunistic behavior. Contrary to suggestions that efforts to reduce leakage of intellectual property undermine the learning potential of alliances, the empirical evidence presented here suggests that firms mitigate "leakage hazards" by crafting alliances that allow partners to credibly commit to jointly beneficial actions.

ORGANIZATION OF THE STUDY

The remainder of the book is organized as follows: Chapter 2 lays out the basic transaction cost model of hybrid organizations in the domestic setting. The focus is on the role of asset specificity as the critical transaction dimension underlying the choice of efficient governance mode, but this is placed in a more general context of "contractual hazards." The equity joint venture, a hybrid archetype, is examined in some detail, and a market-hierarchy continuum is constructed based on a comparative analysis of governance features of various hybrid organizational forms.

Chapter 3 examines contracting hazards related to weak property rights, as they apply to transactions involving the transfer of technology. The severity of appropriability hazards depends on the efficacy of formal instruments of intellectual property protection, and the nature of the activities involved in an alliance (i.e. the transaction characteristics). In the empirical study, a set of hypotheses are developed linking governance choice in alliances with the level of appropriability hazards. Part one of this empirical analysis, on agreements linking US-based firms, is described in Chapter 4.

Chapter 5 moves into the international arena, and describes the added complexity encountered when analyzing international hybrids. A "shift parameter framework" is elaborated, and empirically tested on a sample of alliances involving US and non-US-based firms. The results are consistent with the findings in the US-only analysis, and also show that national differences in intellectual property protection have predictable effects on the organizational form of international hybrids. Chapter 6 summarizes the main findings of the study and discusses their implications for current debates and future research.

TWO

The Market-Hierarchy Continuum of Hybrid Organizations

Hybrid organizations come in many varieties, from long-term supply contracts to joint ventures, franchise arrangements, R&D consortia and complex technology licensing contracts. The idea of organizing these hybrid forms along a "market-hierarchy continuum" is not new: in their book on cooperative strategies in international business, Contractor and Lorange (1988, p. 6) propose a ranking of cooperative ventures based on the degree of "interorganizational dependence," going from least to most hierarchical:

- Technical training and start-up assistance agreements;
- Production, assembly and buy-back agreements;
- Patent licensing;
- Franchising;
- Know-how licensing;
- Management or marketing service agreements;
- Non-equity cooperative agreements in
  - exploration,
  - research partnerships,
  - development/co-production;
- Equity joint ventures.

Although the ordering of some of these organizational forms is quite intuitive (for instance equity joint ventures being more hierarchical, or involving greater organizational interdependence than a patent license), there is much room for debate.[1] Furthermore, it is unclear exactly what "organizational interdependence" entails, absent a systematic dimensionalization of governance (or other critical feature of organization). As demonstrated below, transaction cost economics provides a comparative lens for such a dimensionalization and the development of a theoretically-grounded market-hierarchy continuum of hybrid forms.[2]

TRANSACTION COST ECONOMICS: THE BASIC MODEL

Transaction cost economics (TCE) traces it's origins to the early work of Coase (1937). However, for a long time the theory remained tautological, and has been operationalized only over the past twenty five years. (For a collection of leading articles, see Williamson and Masten, 1995). The theory works out of the behavioral assumptions of bounded rationality and opportunism: Individuals are assumed to be "intendedly rational, but only limitedly so," (Simon, 1961, p. xxiv) which implies that all complex contracts must be incomplete, since explication of all possible contingencies is infeasible. The relevant question then becomes, "given limited competence, how do the parties organize so as to utilize their limited competence to best advantage?" (Williamson, 1985, p. 46). Achieving efficient organization is complicated by actors' potential for opportunistic behavior, or "self-interest seeking with guile" (p. 47),[3] the absence of which would imply that all contractual behavior could be governed by self-enforced promises.

The unit of analysis in TCE is the transaction, where a transaction occurs "when a good or service is transferred across a technologically separable interface" (Williamson, 1992, p. 337). These transactions are described by the attributes of "asset specificity,"[4] uncertainty and frequency. For simple transactions, autonomous market contracts give agents strong incentives to reduce costs, maximize profits, and make efficient adaptations to demand changes signaled through prices. However, certain transactions require investments in special-purpose assets which would lose value should the transaction be prematurely terminated. As this "asset specificity" condition becomes more pronounced, partners to the transaction have a stake in preserving the relationship. The increasingly bilateral character of the contract poses problems, however, as changing circumstances require coordinated adaptation for which autonomous contracts make inadequate provision. Costly haggling over rents is likely to result. In response to (or in anticipation of) these problems, autonomous market contracts are replaced by more complex forms of governance, and ultimately by internal organization. Moving to complex governance structures does incur additional nontrivial set-up costs, and other ongoing costs, however. Therefore, internal organization will be reserved for transactions where asset specificity is high, uncertainty is significant, (so that bilateral adaptation is predictably required) and the frequency of the transaction is sufficient to justify the necessary set-up costs.

The contention of differential organization costs and competencies of market contracts versus internal (hierarchical) organization, rests on the following logic: As suggested above, two types of adaptation may be required in the course of contracting — autonomous adaptation, as effected through the price system,[5] and coordinated or bilateral adaptation in the context of long-term bilateral dependency relations. Autonomous market contracts facilitate autonomous adaptation through high-powered incentives, i.e. the participants are rewarded by appropriating the net receipts associated with their efforts and decisions, where these receipts are readily identified and enforced. Bilateral adaptation, on the other hand, entails cooperation, and this requires that aggressive incentives for local optimization be replaced by lower-powered incentives (e.g. time-rates, cost-based reimbursements, etc.) supported by surveillance and other controls. This is the world of internal organization, or hierarchy, where transactions are subject to administrative controls and direction by fiat.

A key distinguishing feature of hierarchy vs. market controls is the reliance on private ordering vs. legal rules for contract enforcement (Williamson, 1991). In a classic market transaction, disputes are typically resolved by termination of the contract, possibly with damages awarded by the courts. Contracts are narrow and well-specified, as are remedies, and the courts emphasize strict application of the rules of contract law (Macneil, 1978). At the other extreme lies hierarchy, where the transaction takes place within the firm, and dispute settlement is achieved via private ordering. Indeed, courts will refuse to hear disputes between parties within a hierarchy (practicing "forbearance" in Williamsonian terms), and dispute settlement is instead achieved through hierarchical incentive and control systems, with adaptations affected by fiat.

The alignment of transactions with governance structures is the central exercise in transaction cost economics. Table 2.1, below, describes the instruments and adaptive attributes of the polar market and hierarchy forms, with ++ and 0 denoting strong and weak effects.

Figure 2.1 illustrates the logic of the argument for a simple make-or-buy decision. G_m and G_i represent the governance costs[6] for market arrangements (i.e. "buy") and internal organization ("make"), respectively. When asset specificity is negligible, autonomous adaptation only is required, and internal organization imposes unnecessary bureaucratic costs,[7] so a market arrangement (contract) is the preferred governance structure. As asset specificity increases, the cost of market governance increases. Internal governance costs also rise, but at a lower rate. This leads to a threshold level of specificity, k^*, where the governance costs associated with market transactions become

Table 2.1   Attributes of Governance Structures

	Governance Structure	
	Market	*Hierarchy*
Instruments		
Incentive intensity	++	0
Administrative controls	0	++
Contract law	++	0
Performance attributes		
Autonomous adaptability	++	0
Bilateral adaptability	0	++

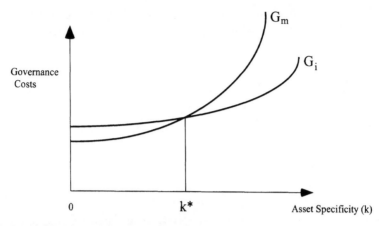

G_m = Governance costs of market arrangement
G_i = Governance costs of internal organization

Figure 2.1   Governance costs and the Boundaries of the firm

of such magnitude that internalization represents the more efficient governance mode.

Asset specificity

Asset specificity conditions that result in contracting hazards may be of several kinds. Williamson (1985) identifies four distinct classes of specificity that have been studied empirically, and have been found to correlate positively with the degree of vertical integration: site specificity, physical asset specificity, dedicated assets and human asset specificity.

Site specificity refers to operations that, for technical reasons, must be located "cheek by jowl." The resulting bilateral dependency between successive production stages makes integration of ownership the most efficient governance arrangement, as observed, for example, in the aluminum industry (Hennart, 1988a; Stuckey, 1983).[8] Similar effects may be observed when investments are made in physical assets that are specialized to the needs of one customer,[9] or when otherwise general-purpose production capacity is dedicated to a particular customer.[10] In each of these cases, finding alternative users or uses for the assets would subsequently incur significant costs and/or loss of asset value. This renders the investor vulnerable to ex-post appropriation of quasi-rents by the customer, perhaps in the form of re-negotiation of the supply contract. The 'market' form of governance under such circumstances also poses hazards for the buyer: farsighted (though boundedly rational) suppliers, anticipating the possibility of ex-post hold-up, are unlikely to make the desired level of investment, except at some elevated (i.e. risk-adjusted) price. Furthermore, after the investments are in place, the buyer is likely to have difficulty in finding alternative forms of supply at the same level of cost and quality. Thus ex-post haggling over the quasi-rents may be initiated by either party to the contract, and the integrated solution is preferred because of the unification of interests that it entails.

The last important class of asset specificity is human asset specificity, which refers to the development of specialized know-how in the context of a particular relationship. Such specialized know-how can develop in many situations. For example, in an employment relationship, employees may develop firm-specific know-how (through training and learning-by-doing) in addition to the 'general purpose' know-how associated with their profession or craft. This firm-specific know-how is often related to the "organizational routines" discussed by Nelson and Winter (1982) and is significant if it has the effect of driving a wedge between the value of this particular employee to this particular firm, and the value to another firm (and/or of an alternative employee). In this instance, it is in the interests of both employer and employee to devise protective employment safeguards.[11]

Other contracting hazards

While backward integration decisions represent the prototypical transaction cost economics puzzle, forward integration into marketing and distribution is also susceptible to analysis through the TCE lens, and human asset specificity is often implicated (Anderson, 1985; Anderson & Schmittlein, 1984; John & Weitz, 1988). In addition, however, forward integration may be in response to contracting hazards related to reputation or brand name capital — where retail outlets are required to provide significant product information or quality guarantees. For example, in the case of consumer durables, where considerable knowledge is imparted at the point of sale, and specialized follow-on service is required, the manufacturer's reputation can be undermined by a dealer who reduces costs by failing to provide these services, undercuts other dealers, and reduces the effective quality of the final good provided (Williamson, 1985). These are essentially externality concerns, where an individual dealer free-rides on the promotional efforts of other retailers, but where the actions of that one dealer negatively impact sales of the product through other outlets, thus degrading the manufacturer's investment in brand name or reputational capital. Forward integration into retailing may be the efficient response in these circumstances (Chandler, 1977).

Another important class of transactions involves horizontal integration decisions. Whereas in vertical transactions one party supplies an input into the other's production activities, horizontal transactions are usually defined as transactions between parties — possibly even competitors — involved in the same range of activities. Transactions involving geographic diversification or horizontal diversification into related industries are salient examples. These horizontal arrangements are particularly prevalent in international business: for example a horizontally integrated multinational enterprise may produce essentially the same line of goods at plants in several countries, or may contract with local companies in some locations to take over the same set of activities that the multinational performs elsewhere. However, the same logic applies to horizontal integration decisions within a single country.

In a horizontal arrangement, the 'problematic' asset typically featured in the transaction is specialized know-how, which may be of several types — technological, managerial, marketing, etc. Asset specificity can still present difficulties in such transactions:

the transaction-specific learning involved in the transfer of technology or know-how assets can lead to high levels of human asset specificity, with the consequent dangers of hold-up. However, a more salient problem for the transferor (seller) of the asset may lie in preventing the transferee (buyer) from taking the technology or other know-how and using it in applications outside the scope of the agreement, without providing appropriate compensation.

Although deficiencies in the "market for know-how," and the difficulties of fully appropriating returns to investment in technological assets have been of interest to researchers for many years (see, for example Arrow, 1962, 1973; Levin et al., 1987; Nelson & Winter, 1982), the implications of the resulting "appropriability hazards" for governance are not fully worked out. This issue is the focus of Chapter 3, but the main point here is that while asset specificity has received the most attention in studies of governance to date, this is just one example (albeit a significant one) of a more general class of "contracting hazards" that governance structures may be designed to overcome or mitigate.

HYBRID ORGANIZATIONS

Of course, in reality, the market and hierarchical governance structures considered so far are merely the polar forms of what is a continuum of possible governance arrangements. We now turn to discussion of a third generic governance form, the "hybrid."

When transactions involve asset specificity or other hazards at intermediate levels, there may be reasons to prefer hybrid governance structures over complete internalization of the transaction. Hybrids are located between markets and hierarchies in their governance attributes, so that the bilateral adaptability features of hierarchy are partially sacrificed in exchange for the autonomous adaptability and incentive intensity features of market or contractual arrangements. Table 2.2 shows the governance instruments and adaptive attributes that distinguish markets, hybrids and hierarchies.

Table 2.2   Hybrids as a Third Generic Form of Governance

	Governance Structure		
	Market	*Hybrid*	*Hierarchy*
Instruments			
Incentive intensity	++	+	0
Administrative controls	0	+	++
Contract law	++	+	0
Performance attributes			
Autonomous adaptability	++	+	0
Bilateral adaptability	0	+	++

++ = strong; + = semi-strong; 0 = weak effect

Table 2.3   Examples of Market, Hybrid and Hierarchy Governance Structures

Activities	*Governance structure*		
	Market	*Hybrid*	*Hierarchy*
Component supply (backward integration)	• Spot market purchasing	• Long-term contract • Co-production agreement • Joint venture	• In-house production
Distribution (forward integration)	• Arms-length distribution contract	• Long-term contract • Reciprocal marketing agreement • Franchise agreement	• Integrated distribution
Diversification or international production (horizontal integration)	• Arms length contract	• Licensing agreement • Second-sourcing agreements • Production JV	• In-house production (including multinational)
R&D	• Open-bid contract	• Complex contract or partnership • R&D consortia • Research JV	• In-house R&D

Examples of hybrid organizations include long-term contracts, franchising, joint ventures, reciprocal trading agreements, and the like. Table 2.3 shows market, hybrid and hierarchy governance structures for a variety of activities.

With high-powered incentives maintained to some extent in these arrangements, the transferee is more likely to utilize assets as efficiently as possible; at the same time, monitoring is facilitated (relative to the level of monitoring feasible within the context of arms-length contracting.) Thus, hybrid modes of organization may offer sufficient protection against opportunism without incurring the full range of bureaucratic costs associated with hierarchy. As such, hybrids will be the preferred mode for transactions with levels of asset specificity in the neighborhood of the (figure 2.1) threshold level $k*$. Figure 2.2 illustrates the heuristic for the choice among market, hybrid and internal organization, when the transaction involves investments in specific assets.

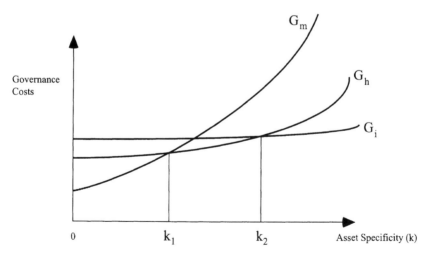

G_m = Governance costs of market arrangement
G_h = Governance costs of hybrid
G_i = Governance costs of internal organization

Figure 2.2   Governance Costs in Market, Hybrid and Hierarchy

The equity joint venture

Although hybrid organizations come in many varieties, the one that has received by far the most attention, particularly in international business research, is the equity joint venture (e.g., Geringer & Hebert, 1989; Gomes-Casseres, 1989; Harrigan, 1986; Hennart, 1988b; Killing, 1983). An equity joint venture is the classic form of hybrid organization, involving the creation of a new entity jointly owned and operated by two or more collaborating firms. Before moving on to a description of the "market-hierarchy continuum" of hybrid forms, it is useful to examine this "hybrid archetype" in more detail.

While there are many descriptions available of the operation and performance of equity joint ventures, most of these are too general to form the foundation of a comparative assessment of other hybrid forms. For example, Pisano et al. (1988) suggest that the administrative hierarchy created in a joint venture allows the parties to set general operational and strategic policies and settle disputes in much the same fashion as occurs in the fully integrated governance mode. At the same time, the governing body of the venture, usually composed of representatives of both companies, can provide a channel for coordinating the collaborative roles of the partners. But what are the critical features of the joint venture that allow this coordination? Is it indeed the presence of a joint board, is it the pooling of financial risks inherent in the equity structure, or is it some other feature? And which of these features can be duplicated in other, contract-based, hybrid organizations? These questions can only be addressed satisfactorily by a systematic analysis of the governance instruments that operate within an equity joint venture. This is best achieved with reference to the three essential categories of governance instruments, shown in Tables 1 and 2: incentive intensity, administrative controls and contract law supports.

Incentive intensity. As discussed earlier, one of the key distinguishing features of market and hierarchy is their respective use of high-powered and low-powered incentives to foster

autonomous adaptation on the one hand and bilateral adaptation on the other. When we examine intermediate governance
structures, the relative strength of the two types of adaptability
depends on (1) the degree to which each party to the transaction retains any surplus generated by its own efforts (i.e. the
power of incentives) and (2) the degree to which the party's
fortunes are tied to the ongoing efficient operation of the venture as a whole (i.e. incentive alignment).

A key process supporting incentive alignment in hybrid
organizations is the exchange of hostages.[12] In most transactions involving investments in specific assets, it is difficult to
perfectly equilibrate the magnitude of the relationship-specific
investments of the two parties to a contract. For example,
many product supply transactions require the supplier to
invest in highly specialized equipment tailored to the needs of
a particular customer in order to minimize production costs,
but no similar investments by the customer may be needed to
support the transaction. Without appropriate safeguards, the
supplier stands to lose if the buyer acts opportunistically and
changes the terms of the exchange after the sunk investments
are in place. A farsighted supplier, recognizing this holdup
problem, will refuse to invest in the specific assets unless additional safeguards are in place.

In a joint venture, the problem just described is mitigated
because of the exchange of hostages achieved by symmetry
(or proportionality) in equity holdings. When a supply
arrangement is organized by setting up an equity joint venture,
each party typically contributes equal monetary investments in
return for equity shares. The pooled financing is then used to
invest in the necessary general purpose and transaction-specific
assets, and the returns are shared according to the equity holdings. Because the value of the shares in the joint venture
depend critically on the continued operation of the enterprise, each firm is effectively posting a bond equal to the
value of the specific investments, since that value will be lost
should operations cease. In cases where partner firms also
make contributions of assets (particularly technology), this

issue is sometimes posed as a question of asset valuation. For example, Mowery and Rosenberg (1989, p. 246) suggest that "partner firms make financial commitments to a collaborative venture that back their claims for the value of the assets they contribute; such financial commitments can substitute for the complete revelation of the value and characteristics of the asset that could be necessary to complete a licensing agreement." Furthermore, as Brodley (1982, p. 1528) argues: "The temptation to exploit a favored bargaining position by threatening to withhold infusions of capital or other contributions is reduced by the need for continuous cooperation if the joint venture is to be effective." Thus, as the ongoing returns to each partner are based on the profits of the venture as a whole (with distributions in proportion to equity shares), the incentives of the two firms in the joint venture are more closely aligned.

The intensity of incentives in a joint venture is not reduced to the same extent as in a fully integrated structure, since parties to the transaction retain a degree of autonomy. However, as in the case of the hierarchical governance structure, the attenuation in incentives requires that other administrative controls take the place of the "discipline of the market," and it is to these that we now turn.

Administrative controls. Administrative controls in a joint venture can take several forms. In addition to the pooling of financial resources, the joint venture also pools managerial control by having a board of directors that typically includes members from partner firms in proportion to equity holdings. This provides a direct communication link with senior management of the parent companies, and is the conduit for directives from partner firms. However, in contrast to the fully integrated solution, these directives are subject to negotiation and compromise if conflicts between the goals and interests of the parent companies arise. Indeed, the right of veto over strategic decisions is often explicitly incorporated in the formal agreement accompanying the creation of a joint venture (Geringer & Hebert, 1989; Killing, 1983).

Joint venture personnel are also usually drawn (at least in part) from the parent company staff. Killing (1983, pp. 26–27) describes the advantages to a parent company in having its personnel in the venture, as follows:

Communication between the venture and the parent company is likely to be improved, simply because employees of the two firms know each other. More complete information offers the prospect of more complete control. Secondly, such an employee is likely to act in ways which the parent would find acceptable, even when his actions are not overtly controlled.

In support of this general proposition, Schaan's (1983) study of joint ventures in Mexico found that:

. . . several other techniques [were] used to ensure the continued loyalty of joint venture personnel.
1. In two of the ten Mexican joint ventures the general manager remained on the parent's payroll.
2. In four ventures the general manager's bonus was tied to one parent's results.
3. In four ventures the general manager was required to attend the parent's worldwide management or technical meetings.
4. In five ventures the promotion and career plans of the general manager were clearly predicated on his returning to the parent company (cited in Killing, 1983, p. 27).

In addition to providing a conduit for communication (in both directions) with the parent companies, this pooling of managerial control also facilitates superior monitoring of the activities of the parties to a transaction (Kogut, 1988). Furthermore, "joint venture owners may be legally entitled to independently verified financial information as well as information acquired through direct observation" (Osborn & Baughn, 1990, p. 505).

Contract law supports.   There are a variety of legal documents accompanying the creation of a joint venture, including the following:

The articles of incorporation, by-laws and shareholders agreements, which are in a legal sense the cornerstone of the venture, [and which] spell out the scope of the venture, the type of decisions which need to come to the board for approval and the percentage of votes needed to approve various types of decision. . . . In addition to these basic agreements, there is often a series of agreements between the joint venture and [the parent companies] which cover the supply of component parts, possibly the marketing of the venture's products. . . and the supply of design and production process technology (Killing, 1983, p. 24)

The need to have a variety of agreements and contracts in addition to the articles of incorporation for a joint venture reflect it's position between the classic contract law that governs contract, and the law of forbearance, which applies to within-firm disputes (where the courts will effectively refuse to intervene). Unless the joint venture faces contract disturbances so great that dissolution (or acquisition by one of the parties) is the preferred course of action, recourse to the courts is not usually feasible for disputes regarding the operation of the joint venture. In this way the contract law supports approach those found in hierarchy. However, in the case of complete breakdown in the parties' commitment to continued operation of the venture, appeal to the courts is still available, to carry out the terms of dissolution or acquisition as set out in the original joint venture agreement.

Additional contractual agreements that govern specific aspects of a joint venture's operations may reinject the law of contract into the venture's governance. However, because of the need for continued cooperation within the joint venture, this is not the rigid blueprint of classical contract law, but rather the highly adjustable framework of neoclassical (or relational) contracting, where third-party arbitration may be called for under certain circumstances, but access to the courts is reserved as a forum of ultimate appeal (Llewellyn, 1931; Williamson, 1985).

Other hybrid modes: governance instruments

In this section, the alternative governance instruments or processes available in other hybrid structures, not involving equity, are described. The performance of these alternatives, relative to each other and to the governance instruments found in joint ventures are assessed.

Incentive intensity.   Incentive intensity (and incentive alignment) in contract-based forms of hybrid organization (i.e. long-term and complex contracts of various types, franchise agreements, technology licensing, R&D agreements, etc.) depends primarily on (i) the design of the compensation scheme; and (ii) the nature and extent of hostage exchange. In the polar market governance form, high-powered incentives are achieved via fixed-price contracts. However, if the nature of the transaction is such that coordination is required, this can result in costly haggling, as discussed earlier in the chapter. Thus, in long-term contracts and other contract-based hybrids, the fixed-price may be supplanted by some type of cost-based contract, such that both parties to the transaction share in any unforeseen cost savings and/or adverse price shocks.[13] Thus incentive intensity is reduced, although not to the same extent as in the case of equity joint ventures, where joint profits are customarily distributed in proportion to equity shares.

Hostage exchanges can also be used in contract-based hybrids to enhance incentive alignment. Recall the case of the customer-supplier relationship, described in the earlier discussion of joint ventures, involving investment in specific assets on the part of the supplier. The simplest hostage arrangement in this case involves the posting of a pecuniary bond by the customer. However, as long as the parties to the contract remain autonomous (so that high-powered incentives are in place) this raises potential problems of contrived cancellation, and difficulties in precisely valuing the specific investments, which is necessary to determine the appropriate bond (Williamson, 1985, pp. 176–78). At best, therefore, pecuniary bonds can provide partial safeguards against expropriation in the context of a unilateral (i.e. goods for cash) contract.

Somewhat more favorable outcomes may be achieved in bilateral contracts involving "safeguards in kind," where the parties to the agreement attempt to equalize their exposure by each investing in specific assets. In the customer-supplier example above, the customer may invest in sales and service systems that only have value in conjunction with servicing final demands for the product produced by the supplier in question. Not only does this guard against opportunistic breach of the contract, but results in correlation of disturbances experienced by the two parties, so that both see opportunities similarly, and coordinated response is thus encouraged. Alternatively, in co-production agreements and the like, where a supplier provides components and the customer performs some of the manufacturing of the final product, symmetry may be attained in specific investments in production technology. Problems in valuation persist, but because the hostages are never exchanged (in contrast to the case of pecuniary bonding) issues of contrived cancellation are avoided. Other examples of such bilateral contracts involving an effective exchange of hostages are reciprocal buying agreements like reciprocal petroleum exchanges and mutual second sourcing agreements, plus technology exchange agreements and joint research agreements.

Administrative controls.   Contract-based hybrid organizations rarely involve even a fraction of the range of administrative controls found in equity joint ventures. When parties to a transaction retain organizational autonomy, control via "fiat" is not an option. Nonetheless, alternative means of facilitating communication and monitoring do exist for other contract-based hybrids. In long-term or single-source supply contracts, for example, there are often specific provisions for monitoring: the buyer, who wishes to monitor the supplier's readiness to provide quality product in a timely and cost-effective manner, has rights to inspect a supplier's facility and gain access to information regarding manufacturing methods, quality control and distribution systems, etc. And in co-production agreements, cross-organizational teams may be formed to facilitate communication and agreement on project scope, activity assignment and progress checks (Shuen, 1994).

The adequacy of these monitoring and communication mechanisms may depend in large part on the type of information required, however: for example, in a long term customer-supplier contract, the supplier's main information need may be for information about future product demand, prospective technology requirements, design changes, etc. These are more difficult to monitor directly, and customer self-reporting is probably inadequate unless additional safeguards are in place to credibly ensure the veracity of such reports. Thus these mechanisms can not completely substitute for the administrative controls available in an equity joint venture or in the hierarchical governance structure.

Contract law supports.   The main distinguishing features of contract-based hybrid organizations with respect to contract-law supports are the extent to which they are governed by classical versus neoclassical contract law (see above). Differences between classical and neoclassical contract law are illustrated in Williamson's discussion of a long-term contract in the coal supply industry: "By contrast with a classical contract, this contract (1) contemplates unanticipated disturbances for which adaptation is needed, (2) provides a tolerance zone...within which misalignments will be absorbed, (3) requires information disclosure and substantiation if adaptation is proposed and (4) provides for arbitration in the event of voluntary agreement fails" (1991, p. 272). Of these, provision for third-party arbitration is a particularly important feature. Such provisions tend to support continuity in trading relations since "one important difference in arbitration and litigation...is that, whereas continuity (or at least completion of the contract) is presumed under the arbitration machinery, that presumption is much weaker when litigation is employed" (Williamson, 1985, p. 71).

THE MARKET-HIERARCHY CONTINUUM

The discussion thus far suggests the following as a relevant list of features to consider when attempting to place a hybrid organization on the "market-hierarchy continuum" — the presence of any of which signifies a shift along the continuum toward hierarchy:

- Does the compensation scheme have cost-based features, or a structured adjustment schedule?
- Is there an effective exchange of hostages? Are these "in kind" safeguards (versus pecuniary bonds)?
- Are there formal monitoring mechanisms and reporting requirements in the contract?
- Are there provisions for shared managerial control?
- Are there provisions for third-party arbitration?
- Is equity shared by the two parties to the transaction?

There are two major obstacles faced when trying to move from this "check list" of features to a unique and exhaustive ranking of hybrid forms. First, if we compare two hybrids in which different combinations of these features are present, how do we weigh the relative importance of the various features to decide which hybrid is more "hierarchical?" Second (and relatedly), different hybrid organizations may be designed to govern different types of activity (as suggested by table 2.3, above). As such, they may embody different and idiosyncratic governance features (such as monitoring mechanisms tailored to the particular informational needs of the parties) or idiosyncratic hostage exchanges that are as much a feature of the activity itself as a feature of the governance structure per se. This is particularly true of technology sharing or research and development, for example, where the pooling of technical resources may have inherent hostage features.

Even within the general class of equity joint ventures, there may be differing degrees of "jointness" — Killing (1983, p. 16), for example, distinguishes among "dominant parent" joint ventures, "shared management" ventures and "independent ventures." Of these, dominant parent ventures are arguably nearest to hierarchy in their governance features, as such ventures "are

MARKET   HIERARCHY

1. Component Supply

- Long term supply contract
- Single source agreement

- Co-production contract

- Customer-supplier joint venture

2. Distribution

- Long term distribution contract
- Franchise agreement

- Reciprocal marketing agreement

- Marketing joint venture

3. International Production/ Horizontal Production Agreements

- Licensing agreement
- Second source agreement

- Cross-licensing
- Technology sharing
- Mutual second sourcing

- Production joint venture

4. Research and Development

- R&D contract

- Joint development agreement
- Joint research pact
- Research consortium (non-equity)

- Research Corporation
- R&D Joint venture

Figure 2.3   The Market-Hierarchy Continuum of Hybrid Forms

managed by their dominant parents virtually as if they are wholly owned subsidiaries." However, this distinction can only be observed with quite detailed information regarding the structure of the organization. This is consistent with the general requirement for microanalytic analysis in transaction cost economics, but can pose a barrier to broad empirical tests of the theory.

Despite these obstacles to generalization, it is possible to construct a market-hierarchy of organizational forms, with the following caveats: (1) only ranking of governance structures within broadly comparable activity classes should be attempted, given the current level of understanding; and (2) hybrid forms should be grouped into "discrete structural alternatives," within which there is undoubtedly significant variation, but for which we can identify "step function" differences in governance attributes, so that we can assign an ordinal ranking to the alternatives. Based on the discussion above, three such alternatives can be identified from simple descriptions of hybrid forms. These are: (a) unilateral long-term contracts, (b) bilateral long-term contracts and (c) equity joint ventures. For the two contract-based hybrid forms, the key distinguishing governance feature is greater incentive alignment in bilateral contracts, based on the ability to effect in-kind hostage exchanges. The sharing of equity in joint ventures further increases incentive alignment, and in addition, there are added administrative controls available in the form of board membership and shared management. Figure 2.3 presents the market-hierarchy continuum for a variety of activity categories.

SUMMARY

The analysis in this chapter suggests that fine-grained comparisons of governance structures require more microanalytic details than are generally available from casual observation of extant organizational forms. However, three discrete forms of hybrid organization can be readily distinguished and rank-ordered along the continuum: unilateral contracts, bilateral contracts and equity joint ventures. While it is acknowledged that there is considerable variation within these governance categories, the differences between categories are of a different order of magnitude.

THREE

Appropriability Hazards and Governance

In the basic transaction cost model outlined in the previous chapter, the primary focus was on the governance implications of contracting hazards resulting from investments in transaction-specific assets — reflecting the emphasis on asset specificity in most work in the transaction cost economics tradition. However, asset specificity is only one example (albeit a significant one) of a more general class of contractual hazards. Indeed, in his most recent statement of the transaction cost economics research agenda, Williamson (1996, p. 3) suggests that: " . . . identification, explication and mitigation of contractual hazards — which take many forms, many of which long went unremarked — are central to the exercise."

In this chapter I examine contracting hazards related to weak property rights, as they apply to transactions involving the transfer of technology. Essentially, the problem is this: A firm possessing intellectual property rights and expertise (or "know-how") in a valuable technological asset may not wish to exploit all potential applications of the technology internally (perhaps because it does not presently possess all the complementary assets or know-how necessary for efficient exploitation of the technology in some applications). One alternative is to transfer (sell) the right to use the technology in these applications to another firm. However for the seller to have confidence in this arrangement, it must be possible to agree upon and enforce a contract which adequately specifies the terms of the transfer. Because a simple contract can be problematic, for reasons explored below, an alternative governance structure involving additional safeguards (or, in the limit, internal organization) may be the preferred solution. The added costs of such a structure are undertaken in the expectation of more secure benefits.

The special contracting problems encountered in technology transactions, arising out of the unique trading characteristics of information, and the consequent failures in the "market for know-how," are introduced below. A survey of the literature assessing the efficacy of intellectual property law suggests that technology does not in fact have the pure public goods characteristics of information. Indeed, in one competing view, transactional difficulties faced in technology transfer are related to the feasibility of effecting know-how transfer across organizational boundaries, rather than to protection of rents (appropriability). Some authors have gone so far as to contend that these "learning" motives render transaction cost economics inadequate for the analysis of inter-firm alliances. Further analysis of the relationship of appropriability and feasibility/learning in technology transfer suggests, however, that the two issues are in fact intimately related and both rely on the formation of governance structures that allow alliance partners to credibly commit to jointly efficient behavior.

THE ECONOMICS OF INFORMATION, AND THE MARKET FOR KNOW-HOW

Perhaps the most influential analysis of the unique trading characteristics of information, or knowledge, is attributed to Arrow (1962, 1971, 1973), who identified a "fundamental paradox" of information — that "its value for the purchaser is not known until he has the information, but then he has in effect acquired it without cost" (1971, p. 152). This paradox suggests the need to establish legally enforceable property rights in information, so that disclosure does not entail "donation" of the property. Indeed, this is the rationale underlying systems of intellectual property protection that exist in various forms throughout the world.

Legal protection of intellectual property does not come without social costs, however. Absent legal protection, information is a pure public good: use can be extended to additional parties at zero cost, consumption by another party does not diminish or degrade the good, and use by additional parties cannot be blocked. Ex post, social welfare is maximized by the widest possible diffusion, which is achieved by transferring the information at marginal cost (effectively zero). This, of course, does not allow for rewarding the "producers" or discoverers of the information, so the challenge is to balance the need to provide incentives to invest in inventive activity against the desire for widespread diffusion of the information once it is discovered. This balancing feat has occupied policy analysts, lawyers and economists for decades, and has led to a rich literature on the design of "optimal" intellectual property rules (e.g., Chang, 1991; Gilbert & Shapiro, 1990; Klemperer, 1990; Merges & Nelson, 1992; Scotchmer, 1991), but there remains little consensus on what such optimal rules should be in practice, and significant variation in rules adopted by nations around the globe persists. Furthermore, as discussed below, the efficacy of intellectual property protection varies considerably across industrial sectors.

Intellectual property protection: rules and limits

In a survey of firms' assessments of intellectual property protection, Mansfield (1994, p. 5) found that "there is little correlation between one industry's evaluation of the strength or weakness of intellectual property protection...and another industry's evaluations of [protection] in the same country." A first step to understanding why this is the case is to look at what legal instruments are available for the protection of intellectual property, and what the requirements are for obtaining such protection.[1]

The patent is the most widely used instrument of intellectual property protection for industrial technology. In the US, patents are awarded to inventors of tangible products or processes that are shown to be novel, useful and nonobvious.[2] A patent creates an exclusive right, for a finite time period, to make, use and sell the patented invention. In order to be granted a patent, the inventor must be able to articulate the design in sufficient detail to enable someone proficient in the art to construct the product. Patents therefore provide the most effective protection for technologies that are codifiable, and where imitation is easily observed and verified by the courts.

Trade secrets are another important way to protect intellectual property, although the legal protection provided is very limited. Trade secrets (as defined in intellectual property rules) cover a vast array of technical, commercial and other business material, including formulas, manufacturing processes, product specifications, marketing plans, customer lists, etc. Trade secret law provides the owner of a trade secret with legal protection against unauthorized use or disclosure of the secret by anyone to whom the secret is revealed on a confidential basis (e.g. employees, joint venture partners or licensees), and anyone who obtains the secret through theft or deception. However, the protection is limited in scope. A trade secret owner is not protected against duplication of the secret by legitimate, independent innovation, or against use by third parties who innocently learn of the secret; in other words, once a trade secret has been publicly disclosed, the cat cannot be put back in the bag. Trade secrets are therefore a less secure form of intellectual property than patents. Other legal instruments of some relevance are copyright, which is an important instrument for protection of computer software, and specialized protection such as provided for in the US by the Semiconductor Chip Protection Act of 1984, combining elements of patent and copyright.

In a series of empirical studies on patents and innovation, Mansfield (1985, 1986, 1993, 1994; see also Mansfield, Schwartz & Wagner, 1981) analyzed how firms and industries differ in their propensity to patent, as well as in how rapidly new technological information leaks out, and in the average level of imitation costs (with and without patent protection). The main findings from these studies are that patents are regarded as essential to the development or introduction of a significant proportion of products in the pharmaceutical and chemical industries. Patents are less important, however, in petroleum, machinery and fabricated metal products and of little significance in electrical equipment, office equipment, motor vehicles, instruments, primary metals, rubber and textiles.[3] This difference does not arise simply because innovations in the latter group of industries do not fulfill patenting requirements: over 80 percent of the patentable inventions in the industries where patents are deemed "important" were patented, compared with about 60 percent in the other industries.

One possible reason for the inter-industry variation in the importance of patents is the speed with which technological information leaks out to rivals. According to firms surveyed by Mansfield (1985), information concerning the decision to develop a new product or process is generally in the hands of at least some rivals within about 12 to 18 months. However, inter-industry differences are small, as Mansfield points out: "...with the exception of processes in a few industries like chemicals, there seems to be little difference among industries in the rate of diffusion of such information" (p. 221). The one clear characteristic that is identified as affecting the rate of information leakage is whether the new technology development is for a product or process: "Because new processes can be developed with less communication and interaction with other firms than new products, process development decisions tend to leak out more slowly than product development decisions in practically all industries" (p. 219).

Of course the rate of diffusion of technological information to rivals does not in itself determine how fast innovations can be imitated. In a study of imitation costs in the chemical, drug, electronics and machinery industries,[4] Mansfield et al. (1981) found considerable variation in the time and cost of imitation, but little systematic inter-industry variation overall. However, inter-industry differences were significant for the amount by which patent protection increased imitation costs: average imitation cost increases attributed to patent protection were 30% in ethical drugs, in contrast to 10% in chemicals and about 7% in electronics and machinery. This industry ranking is consistent with the previously discussed findings on the importance of patents in different industries.

The puzzle remains: if patent protection is so much more effective in certain industries (and these industries patent more frequently), why is imitation not achieved more easily in those industries where patents are not effective? Mansfield et al. (1981, p. 910) suggest the following reason:

> It may come as a surprise that imitation cost was no smaller than innovation cost in about one seventh of the cases. This was not due to any superiority of the imitative product over the innovation. Instead, in a substantial percentage of these cases, it was due to the innovator's having a technological edge over its rivals in the relevant field. Often this edge was due to superior "know-how" - specialised experience with the development and production of related products and processes. Such know-how is not divulged in patents and is relatively inaccessible (at least for a period of time) to potential imitators.

The picture that emerges is one where information about a technological innovation leaks out to potential rivals quite quickly in most industries, but where that information may not be easily or costlessly used by rivals, either because patents are effective (i.e. easy to obtain and enforce) or because much of the know-how embodied in the innovation is not easily accessed by outsiders, particularly when rivals are not on technological parity.

Technology transfer and appropriability hazards

Although often characterized as such, it is now apparent that "technology" is not synonymous with pure "information," and does not always have the same public good features as information. In an insightful review of the treatment of technological know-how in the economics literature, Nelson (1990, pp. 1–2) highlights the different perspectives on what is public and what is private about technology:

> In... production theory as presented in the textbooks, the presumption almost always is that technology is a public good. In... models considering the economic consequences of patents... technology is treated as a "latent" public good in that it is presumed that were others permitted to use it they could do so at zero real cost of

technology transfer. The literature on "spillovers"... also sees technology as a latent public good, with patent or other protection porous, thus permitting some of it to become manifestly public. On the other hand, there is a body of research on learning curves and... technology transfer... that dilutes or denies that technology is even a latent public good by highlighting the real cost involved when a firm seeks to acquire effective control of a technology even when there is open access.

Arguments in the technology transfer and learning literature (e.g., Behrman & Wallender, 1976; Robinson, 1988; Teece, 1977) rest on the notion of technology as having a significant "tacit" component, where "a new technology is a complex mix of codified data and poorly defined 'know-how'" (Mowery & Rosenberg, 1989, p. 7). This literature emphasizes the difficulties encountered by firms when they try to acquire technology via an arms-length contract. Codified data, which can be laid out in a set of "blueprints" (and described in a contract), is only part of the "package" that must be transferred in order for the receiving firm to be able to successfully implement the new technology. The other part — the "poorly defined know-how" — cannot be codified, nor fully articulated. This tacit know-how is "extremely difficult to transfer without intimate personal contact, involving teaching, demonstration and participation" (Teece, 1985, p. 29).

Achieving the necessary involvement on the part of the transferor of technology in a contractual relationship may be problematic because of difficulties in specifying (or even knowing in advance) precisely what will be required to achieve effective transfer of the know-how. Furthermore, "it will often not suffice just to transfer individuals. While a single individual may sometimes hold the key to much organizational knowledge, group support is often needed, since organizational routines (Nelson & Winter, 1982, ch. 5) may need to be transferred" (Teece, 1985, p. 29). Important factors affecting the feasibility of technology transfer identified in these studies include the complexity and age of the technology (since new technologies tend to be less well codified), the technological capabilities of the recipient firm — its "absorptive capacity" (Cohen & Levinthal, 1990) — and the amount of previous experience the firms have with technology transfer. These factors together determine the need for training, demonstration and personnel transfers and the associated difficulties in writing and enforcing contracts for technology transfer, as discussed below.

THE 3-STAGE "MODEL" OF APPROPRIABILITY HAZARDS

It is important to make the distinction here between discussions of appropriability that refer to leakage of information to (and imitation by) rivals, and appropriability hazards that arise in the course of contracting for the use of an asset, since the same logic cannot necessarily be applied in each case. In his discussion of "appropriability regimes," for example, Teece (1986, p. 287) argues that a high degree of "tacitness" of the know-how embodied in a technological innovation reduces appropriability hazards, because inventing around a patent is more difficult in this case. However, if we consider the effect of tacit know-how on the ease of contracting, it becomes apparent that the argument does not carry through: if parties attempt to contract for the right to use a technological asset embodying significant tacit know-how, they will encounter serious obstacles to specifying in a contract the asset and the associated property or usage rights to be transferred. Thus, while the tacitness of know-how reduces appropriability hazards with respect to unrelated parties, hazards in contracting for the transfer of the asset are actually increased.

Teece's (1986) treatment of appropriability highlights another challenge facing researchers in this area: he defines the appropriability regime as "the environmental factors, excluding firm and market structure, that govern an innovators ability to capture profits generated by an innovation" (p. 287). The problem with this definition is that it is a composite of features of the technology, the industry and the intellectual property laws in effect. As such, it is difficult to operationalize the concept and apply it to an assessment of appropriability hazards in a particular transaction. The solution is to think about the "appropriability problem" in contracts for the use of technology as a three stage process: (i) specification of intellectual property rights; (ii) monitoring and; (iii) enforcement.

In order to write a simple contract for the use of a technology, it is first necessary to specify, in detail, the property rights involved, i.e. what, precisely, is the asset that is being transferred, what rights of use, modification and/or resale are (and are not) intended in the contract, etc. The ease with which these rights can be specified is largely a function of the type of asset involved. At the most basic level, if the contract is designed to govern the creation rather than the exploitation of technology (as is the case in an R&D contract, for example), specification will inevitably be problematic, since the assets do not exist at the time the contract is written, and technological innovation is a highly uncertain process (Freeman, 1982; Mowery & Rosenberg, 1989).

Even for existing assets, specification is not necessarily straightforward. As suggested above, the degree of "tacitness" of know-how is one relevant consideration: since tacit know-how is, by definition, difficult to articulate, precise specification in a contract of the relevant intellectual property rights is impossible for highly tacit know-how. Which technologies will have the highest degree of "tacitness" is an empirical question — no simple predictive rules can be derived from theory. Luckily, previous studies suggest some relevant distinctions. First, process technologies are often characterized as involving highly tacit know-how.[5] Technologies that are integral components in complex systems may also be more difficult to fully specify (and measure). As Levin et al. (1987, p. 798) suggest:

The most probable explanation for the robust finding that patents are particularly effective in chemical industries is that comparatively clear standards can be applied to assess a chemical patent's validity and defend against infringement. The uniqueness of a specific molecule is more easily demonstrated than the novelty of, for example, a new component of a complex electrical or mechanical system... To the extent that very simple mechanical inventions approximate molecules in their discreteness and easy differentiability, it is understandable that industries producing such machinery rank just after chemical industries in the perceived effectiveness of patent protection.

The age of a technology is also an important factor: contracts are more difficult to specify for novel technologies (particularly those embodying a radical change from previous methods) because the buyer and seller will share even less of the tacit know-how associated with its application than is usual for more "routine" innovations (Davidson & McFetridge, 1984).

Specification of property rights is not in itself sufficient to ensure the security of a contract for the use of an asset: If the owner of the intellectual property is to have confidence that the users of the asset will confine their activities to those provided for in a licensing agreement, they must be able to monitor the scope of those activities, and enforce the terms of the agreement. The magnitude of monitoring requirements will again depend on the nature of the technology and activities involved in the transaction. If the know-how transferred is embodied in a product design, then monitoring of the product offerings of the licensee should be sufficient to assess compliance. If, on the other hand, the license is for process technology, it may be impossible to discern its use by simple observation of outputs: the licensee may exploit the technology in a product area outside the scope of the agreement without notifying or compensating the owner of the intellectual property.

Even when a violation of a licensing agreement is detected, enforcing intellectual property rights can be difficult, as suggested in the discussions of the efficacy of intellectual property protection, above. Some of these problems certainly are rooted in difficulties in property right specification (and thus the three stages of the appropriability hazard problem should not be interpreted as mutually exclusive). "Inventing around" patents is a common problem in some industries, and has been the basis of countless patent infringement suits. Other problems are related to the difficulties of third-party verifiability of the licensee's actions, as required by the court. Enforcement difficulties are particularly problematic in the international arena, due to significant cross-national differences in intellectual property laws — an issue that is taken up in the international empirical analysis in Chapter 5.

Implications for governance

Most product transactions today involve technology in some form and, in most cases, classical market arrangements (i.e. spot contracts) work well. However, difficulties encountered at any of the three stages of contracting for technology — specification of intellectual property rights, monitoring, or enforcement — will lead to an increase in appropriability hazards, and a move towards more hierarchical forms of organization. The governance features of hierarchy work to mitigate appropriability hazards in several ways: lower-powered incentives (and alignment of incentives with the seller) reduce the likelihood that the buyer will violate the terms of the agreement; the administrative controls available within hierarchy increase the ability to monitor the activities undertaken in the course of the agreement and allow greater direction of those activities; and the reduced reliance on court ordering for dispute resolution (in the limit, forbearance) decreases the requirements for third party verifiability. These benefits do not come without cost, however. Attenuated incentives mean that the technology may not be exploited in its best use, or to its fullest extent. Thus internal organization will be reserved for cases in which contractual hazards are at their height, and a hybrid governance structure may be the preferred solution for transactions with "mid range" appropriability hazards. This point is particularly relevant when development of a composite technology requires that diverse elements be brought together, and these are not currently found within a single firm. In this case, internal development implies acquisition or merger of a number of firms that together own all of the necessary technologies. A hybrid organization which approaches hierarchy (i.e. an equity joint venture) may be the preferred governance mode in this case. Figure 3.1 summarizes the assignment of transactions to governance structures to mitigate appropriability hazards, based on the logic of the 3-stage model of the appropriability problem.

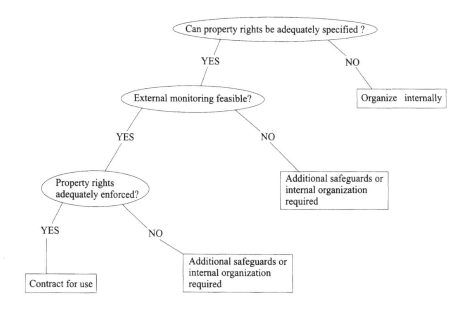

Figure 3.1   Appropriability Hazards and Governance

LEARNING VERSUS "LEAKAGE"

Before moving on to empirical testing of the theoretical framework developed above, it is important to acknowledge some potentially competing explanations of the emergence and structure of inter-firm alliances. For example, Kogut and Zander (1992, 1993, 1996) have developed a "knowledge-based" theory of the firm in which they argue that the degree of know-how tacitness increases the differential cost of transferring information across firm boundaries because of the need for a "common code" embedded in operating routines of the transferor and transferee. Thus, for the choice between a contract-based and equity joint venture, Kogut (1998, p. 323) suggests that joint ventures are the preferred vehicle by which tacit knowledge is transferred, and other contractual forms of transfer are ruled out, "not because of market failure or high transaction costs as defined by Williamson and others, but rather because the very knowledge being transferred is organizationally embedded."

This argument, which does not rely on opportunism of the partners in an alliance, is apparently at odds with the transaction cost framework described so far. However, closer examination of the underlying logic reveals that, while offering many important insights into the process of (and obstacles to) know-how transfer within and between firms, Kogut and Zander's argument falls short of explaining the choice among different governance alternatives for inter-firm alliances. For the choice between an equity joint venture and a contract for effecting technology transfer, for example, the two firms sharing technology cannot be assumed to share "codes" in either case since they are, by definition, autonomous firms. So, where do the advantages of an equity joint venture lie? Kogut and Zander argue that overcoming difficulties in transferring tacit know-how requires that personnel are co-located for a nontrivial time period to facilitate learning by doing, demonstration, feedback, etc. Indeed, support for this premise can be found in previous studies of the direct costs of technology transfer within and between multinational firms (Teece, 1977, 1981), as well as in studies indicating that inter-partner knowledge transfer is greater in equity joint ventures than in contract-based alliances (Mowery, Oxley, & Silverman, 1996).

The question remains, however, why is the necessary co-location of personnel most effectively achieved within an *equity joint venture*? After all, absent opportunism, the two firms could simply write a general clause contract agreeing to pool personnel, perhaps in a separate facility (as is often the case with an equity joint venture), and to share know-how and distribute benefits based on some pre-agreed sharing rule. In reality, it is apparent that such an arrangement is fraught with hazards related to the misappropriation of know-how (or hold-up in the face of relationship-specific investments). And it is precisely the governance features of the equity sharing and joint management in a joint venture that mitigate these hazards and imbue the relationship with the confidence necessary for significant know-how sharing and consequent "learning."

A related explanation of the benefits of a joint venture versus a license is that licensees are always "less capable" of technology absorption or learning than are joint venture partners (implicit, for example, in Hill, Hwang, & Kim, 1990). This argument may be plausible in comparisons of transfers internal to the firm and those to potential licensees — in this case, it is reasonable to argue that "through repeated interactions, individuals and groups in a firm develop a common understanding by which to transfer knowledge..." (Kogut & Zander, 1993, p. 631) and that this makes knowledge transfers within the group more effective than is possible with any "new" licensee. However, when considering the choice of collaborative mechanism, one can (and should) keep the identity of the collaborating partners constant across alternatives. Thus we see that the advantages of one structure (e.g., a joint venture) over another (e.g., a contract) must rest on organizational and governance features, not on the identity or characteristics of partner firms.

FOUR

An Empirical Study of Appropriability Hazards in International Strategic Alliances Stage 1: US-Based Firms

In this chapter and in Chapter 5, I report the results from a two-stage empirical study of appropriability hazards in international strategic alliances. Specifically, I address the following research questions: When two or more firms decide to form a strategic alliance for the development and/or exploitation of technology, how is the particular mode of cooperation chosen? How do appropriability hazards affect this choice? What attributes of the project (transaction), the partner firms and the national setting determine the level of appropriability hazards?

A basic premise of this research is that international strategic alliances are susceptible to the same analytical framework as domestic alliances, albeit with some extensions. The empirical study was therefore designed to be conducted in two-stages: Stage 1 (presented in this chapter) examines domestic and global alliances between US-based firms only,[1] and Stage 2 of the study (in Chapter 5) analyzes alliances between firms of different nationalities.

The principal source of data for the study is the Cooperative Agreements and Technology Indicators (CATI) information system, a relational database covering over 9,000 cooperative agreements involving parent companies in many countries. The organizational form of each agreement is identified in the database, allowing placement on the "market-hierarchy continuum" of inter-firm alliances. The severity of appropriability hazards is modeled as a function of the type of transaction, the geographic and technological scope of the activities governed by the alliance, and the strength of protection of intellectual property rights. Discrete choice methods are used to test the hypothesis that greater appropriability hazards lead firms to choose more hierarchical types of alliance. Results from an examination of horizontal production alliances involving US-based firms provide strong support for this hypothesis: more hierarchical alliances are chosen when technology is difficult to specify, and when the scope of activities is wider, so that monitoring of activities is hampered. Thus, as appropriability hazards increase, unilateral licensing agreements give way to cross-licensing agreements, and eventually to equity joint ventures.[2]

Inclusion of firm-level variables in the empirical model illuminates a source of confusion in previous empirical studies. In the international management literature, empirical studies of governance choice in inter-firm alliances increasingly rely on the logic of transaction cost economics (Agarwal & Ramaswami, 1992; Gomes-Casseres, 1989; Hennart, 1991; Hladik, 1985) but almost without exception, these studies use firm-level characteristics (R&D spending, advertising, firm size, etc.) to proxy for the transaction-level characteristics featured in TCE. This mismatch between the underlying phenomenon and the empirical measures is reflected in inconsistencies in the observed effects of firm-level variables in these previous studies.[3] In the empirical analysis reported here, firm-level characteristics do not have statistically significant effects. This confirms that, in line with transaction cost theory, it is attributes of the transaction (i.e. the project), and not those of the firm as a whole, that determine the more efficient mode of governance in alliances.

HYPOTHESES

The starting point for the empirical analysis is the proposition, developed in Chapter 3, that if appropriability hazards are present to a sufficient degree, contractual relationships should give way to hybrid or (in the limit) hierarchical forms of organization. Where we are concerned with the choice of mode *within* the general class of hybrid organizations (or strategic alliances), this logic can be summarized in the following proposition: *More hierarchical alliance modes will be chosen in the presence of greater appropriability hazards, i.e. when property right security is uncertain, and 'leakage' would result in significant loss of value.*

Development of testable hypotheses for the empirical analysis requires that this proposition be operationalized, by identifying those characteristics of the transaction, the participating firms and/or the institutional environment which the theory posits will lead to increased appropriability hazards, and thus to adoption of a more hierarchical alliance form. The three aspects of the "appropriability problem" identified in Chapter 3 — property right specification, monitoring and enforcement — facilitate this, since increases in the difficulty or cost of any of the identified features leads to greater appropriability (contracting) hazards and the adoption of a more hierarchical mode of governance.

Specification

It was previously argued that the ease with which property rights can be specified will depend on whether the purpose of the alliance is the creation or exploitation of technological assets, plus the age/novelty and the degree of "tacitness" of the know-how embodied in the technology. Information on the age of a technology and direct measures of "tacitness" are not obtainable in the kind of dataset used in this empirical analysis. We can nonetheless draw some inference about the ease or difficulty of property rights specification from the types of activities involved in the alliance.

In Chapter 2, the case was made that ordering of hybrid organizations along a governance continuum can only be undertaken *within* certain general activity categories. Direct comparisons across categories are not valid, given the current state of understanding, without considerable additional microanalytic data. Specifically, it is important to distinguish vertical from horizontal relationships, and to separate R&D activities from the more "routine" organizational activities of product design, production and marketing. Thus, in the empirical analysis, we restrict our attention to horizontal technology transfer alliances. Such alliances are primarily concerned with the exploitation of existing technologies, but they nonetheless may involve product or process design, production and marketing, or some mixture of these activities. Among these different "transaction types," those which include design activities are most likely to involve the creation or significant modification of technology, so raising the difficulty of adequate specification of contractual terms. Alliances involving these activities are therefore expected to present greater appropriability hazards than are "pure" production and marketing agreements, and hence adoption of a more hierarchical governance structure is predicted, ceteris paribus.

H1: A more hierarchical governance mode will be chosen when an alliance involves product or process design than when only production or marketing activities are undertaken.

Monitoring

While monitoring is essentially a governance attribute in the TCE model, there are aspects of the transaction that affect the adequacy of the "external" monitoring feasible within the context of a contractual (i.e., non-equity) relationship. For example, increases in the number of products or technologies included in a contract, or increases in the geographic scope of the transaction, will inevitably increase the difficulty and cost of monitoring activities (as well as possibly exacerbating specification problems). Similarly, if a contract is used to govern a project involving multiple firms, monitoring costs will increase with the number of partners, as assigning accountability for actions taken by multiple partners under uncertainty is problematic (Alchian & Demsetz, 1972). This suggests that the scope of the transaction should be limited unless there are compelling reasons to do otherwise, for example because of the need to bring together diverse elements in a single project. Where increased scope is necessary, a more hierarchical governance structure is indicated. Thus, we have:

H2: A more hierarchical governance structure will be chosen for transactions involving a broader range of products or technologies.

H3: A more hierarchical governance structure will be chosen for transactions covering a wider geographic area.

H4: A more hierarchical governance structure will be chosen when there are more firms involved in a transaction.

Enforcement

As well as affecting monitoring, increased geographic scope of an alliance may also increase enforcement difficulties, if property rights must be enforced through the courts, and regulations differ among countries. In general, however, for alliances between firms based in the same country, disputes over intellectual property will be decided in the home country (i.e., in US courts for alliances between US firms, even if the alliance covers operations around the globe). Thus, for Stage 1 of the empirical analysis, involving US-based firms only, we would not expect there to be systematic differences in the ability to enforce technology contracts, other than those related to inherent characteristics of the transaction (e.g. tacitness and related difficulties in third-party verification of technology transfers).[4] Issues of differential enforcement of intellectual property rights play a much more significant role in border-crossing alliances (involving firms from more than one country), as demonstrated in the Stage 2 empirical results presented in Chapter 5.

Alternative safeguards

Within the governance continuum framework, the focus is on those governance features that are "built-in" to the various types of hybrid organization. However, in certain instances, the relationship between transaction characteristics and the governance structure adopted may be influenced by the presence of alternative safeguards that can act as partial substitutes for more formal governance instruments. One such alternative safeguard is the exchange of hostages involved when firms are linked in multiple ongoing alliances. If the parties to an alliance are involved in other alliances together (whether contractual or equity-based), then the payoff to opportunism within each alliance is lowered, because of the risk that continued gains to cooperation in all of the alliances will be withdrawn (Gulati, 1995a; Kogut, 1989). Alternatively, repeat alliances may reduce adverse selection problems in partner choice because of improved information developed over the course of previous cooperative projects (whether ongoing or not), regarding a partner's technological capabilities, assets and behavior (Balakrishnan & Koza, 1993). Thus, we have:

H5: Less hierarchical governance modes will be chosen if the partners are involved in multiple alliances together.

DATA SOURCE

The principal source of alliance data is the Cooperative Agreements and Technology Indicators (CATI) information system. Cooperative agreements in the CATI database are defined as "common interests between independent (industrial) partners which are not connected through (majority) ownership," and all involve some arrangement for technology transfer or joint research (Hagedoorn, 1993, p. 377).

The CATI data is based on systematic examination of secondary reports of alliance formation, primarily during the 1980s. In addition to the organizational form of the alliance, the database includes information on the identity and nationality of the partners, the date of establishment, the type and scope of the transaction involved, and the industry, or technology sector in which the cooperative agreement takes place. Coverage of the overall population of global alliances is inevitably incomplete, and there are significant biases in the data, particularly with respect to geographic and industrial sectors covered.[5] Such biases and omissions arguably render the data unsuitable for analysis of aggregate alliance activity or of firms' propensity to form strategic alliances. However, conversations with the originators of the data and independent verification of data on a random sample of alliances confirm that there are no systematic biases in the description and coding of alliance form and activities. Thus, the reported biases are not critical here, where we examine individual decisions regarding the choice of organizational form.

MODEL AND ESTIMATION RESULTS

Empirical sample

The primary sample for analysis comprises all horizontal technology transfer alliances between public US-based manufacturing firms in the CATI database, established during the period 1980–89: a total of 165 alliances. Restricting the analysis to public firms undoubtedly introduces some bias into the sample, as many of the smallest firms will be excluded. This is unavoidable, however, since the firm-specific information necessary for analysis of the "complete" model, including control variables, is not readily available for private companies (see variable list, below). In order to assess whether the restricted sample materially affects the results, a simplified model was also estimated for a larger sample of alliances which included private and non-manufacturing firms. This sample comprises 507 alliances, and the model includes only those variables available from CATI.

Dependent variable

The dependent variable comes from the "market-hierarchy continuum" of hybrid forms, developed in Chapter 2. Three ordered categories of alliance forms were distinguished on that continuum, going from least to most hierarchical: (i) unilateral contractual agreements; (ii) bilateral contractual agreements; and (iii) equity arrangements. For the sample of horizontal technology transfer alliances, the dependent variable (FORM) thus takes on one of three values:

FORM = 0, for unilateral contractual technology transfer alliances, i.e. for licensing and second sourcing agreements;

FORM = 1, for bilateral contractual technology transfer alliances, i.e. for cross-licensing, mutual second sourcing and technology sharing agreements;

FORM = 2, for equity-based technology transfer alliances, i.e. equity joint ventures.

To briefly recap the logic underlying this ordering; moving from unilateral to bilateral contractual agreements facilitates incentive alignment because of the reciprocal nature of the arrangement, which effectively involves an "exchange of hostages." This makes each firm dependent on the other for continued benefits of cooperation and reduces the incentives for either partner to violate the terms of the agreement. Moving to an equity arrangement (i.e., joint venture) further increases this bilateral dependence and incentive alignment, and also facilitates monitoring and enhanced administrative control.

Independent variables

A list of independent variables is shown in table 4.1, with the relevant sources, and hypothesized signs. All firm-specific information is derived from Compustat data[6] and table 4.2 presents the means, standard deviations and range of values for the independent variables in the sample of 165 alliances between public US-based firms. None of these variables are highly correlated: the largest correlation coefficient is 0.601, between alliance experience and average size of alliance partners.

The number of partners was excluded as an independent variable for analysis of the "public firm" sample of 165 alliances, as there were only two alliances in this sample having more than two partners.[7] The number of partners is reintroduced in the model for the full sample of 507 firms, however. The overlapping alliances variable (a measure of alternative safeguards) is the number of alliances in the CATI database established prior to the establishment date of the alliance in question and involving all of the same partner firms.

Table 4.1 Independent Variables for Stage 1 Analysis

Variable	Definition	Source	Predicted sign
Transaction Type	Activities covered by agreement: product/ process design, production/ marketing or "mixed."	CATI	+
Technology Scope	Products or technologies covered: one, a few or many.	CATI	+
Geographic Scope	Geographic scope of alliance: USA, N. America or worldwide	CATI	+
Number of Partners	Number of firms in alliance	CATI	+
Overlapping Agreements	Number of alliances linking partner firms, established prior to this alliance	CATI	−
Control Variables:			
Industry	CATI technology sectors — biotech, info tech, new materials and "other"	CATI	n/a
Average Firm Size	Average size of alliance partners (total assets in millions of 1980 dollars)	Compustat	n/a

Table 4.1   (*contd.*)

Variable	Definition	Source	Predicted sign
Relative Size	Ratio of smallest firm to largest firm, measured by total assets	Compustat	n/a
Average R&D	Combined R&D intensity of alliance partners (total R&D spending/total sales)	Compustat	n/a
R&D Gap	Maximum difference among partners' R&D spending/sales	Compustat	n/a
Same Industry	Coded 1 if "main 4-digit SIC" is same for all alliance partners	Compustat	n/a
Venturing Experience	Average number of alliances of partner firms, prior to this alliance establishment date	CATI	n/a

Table 4.2   Descriptive Statistics for Independent Variables, Stage 1

	Mean	Std. Dev.	Minimum	Maximum
Design Transaction Dummy 1 = design 0 = production or mixed	0.078	0.269	0	1
Mixed Transaction Dummy 1 = mixed 0 = production or design	0.120	0.326	0	1
Technology Scope 1 = few or broad range of technologies or products 0 = single technology or product	0.365	0.483	0	1

Geographic Scope 1 = Global Operations 0 = USA or N. America	0.267	0.444	0	1
Overlapping Agreements = number of alliances linking partner firms	2.018	1.684	1	9
Information Technology Dummy	0.491	0.501	0	1
Biotechnology Dummy	0.150	0.358	0	1
New Materials Dummy	0.126	0.333	0	1
Average Size = average size of partners (total assets, in $millions)	11.20	14.55	0.036	77.18
Asset ratio = total assets of smallest partner/total assets of largest partner	0.234	0.256	0.001	0.997
Combined R&D intensity = total R&D spending/ total sales	0.062	0.041	0.003	0.259
R&D Gap = largest difference among partners' R&D spending/sales	0.136	0.371	0.01	2.524
Same Industry 1 = all partners in same 4-digit SIC 0 = otherwise	0.120	0.326	0	1
Alliance Experience = average total number of alliances of partner firms prior to this alliance date	16.50	13.49	0	65
Time Trend	5.46	2.57	0	9

In addition to the independent variables featured in the hypotheses, the following control variables are included in the model:

Technology/research field or industry. A series of dummy variables are included, based on the "core technology sectors" identified in the CATI database: "information technology," "new materials" and "biotechnology." Observations without a dummy variable attached are all other technology sectors represented in the CATI data.[8] This variable controls for significant sectoral differences in the propensity to enter into certain types of alliances that are not captured in the transaction or firm-level independent variables.

Firm size. Previous studies of the decision to enter joint ventures, and studies of joint venture performance, have included among the independent variables, the absolute size of the firm, (e.g., Agarwal & Ramaswami, 1992; Gomes-Casseres, 1990) and/or the asymmetry in the size of participating firms (Harrigan, 1988; Hennart, 1991). Average size (measured as total assets in 1982 dollars) of the partner firms in the alliance, and the "size ratio" of the firms (i.e. the total assets of the smallest firm in the alliance divided by the total assets of the largest firm) are therefore included in the model.[9]

R&D intensity. The combined R&D intensity (i.e. total R&D spending/total revenues) of the partner firms is included as a control, since R&D intensity has been a significant (though not consistent) explanatory variable in previous studies of joint venturing versus autonomous international investment (Agarwal & Ramaswami, 1992; Gomes-Casseres, 1989; Hennart, 1991; Kogut & Chang, 1991).

R&D Gap. A relevant finding from the technology transfer literature is that a large "capabilities gap" between the technology donor and recipient firms increases the costs of transferring technology across firm boundaries (Teece, 1981). R&D gap, measured as the absolute value of the largest difference in the R&D intensities of partner firms is therefore included as a proxy to control for the potential impact of such a "capabilities gap."

Partners in same industry. Also following previous studies, (e.g., Balakrishnan & Koza, 1993; Gomes-Casseres, 1989; Hennart, 1991) a control dummy is included that captures whether both (or all) alliance partners have their primary operations in the same industry (at the 4-digit SIC level).

Alliance experience. If experience in alliances lowers governance costs more for certain modes than for others, then total alliance experience may affect the choice of mode. A control variable was constructed based on the average number of alliances (in the CATI database) established by each partner firm prior to the establishment date of the alliance in question. Although this measure is inevitably biased over time, this likely reflects the actual experience of firms in the sample, since technology-related alliances were not a common feature of firm strategy prior to the 1980s (Contractor & Lorange, 1988).

Time trend. To capture any systematic change in alliance structures adopted over time, an annual time trend is included, which takes a value of 0 for alliances established in 1980, to 9 for alliances established in 1989.

Statistical methodology

As discussed above, the unit of observation for the analysis is the alliance. Because the categorical dependent variable can take on one of three ordered values, ordered probit is used for the statistical analysis.[10] The model is specified as follows:

$$(1) \quad z_i = \beta X_i + \varepsilon_i,$$

where z_i is an unobservable measure of the position of alliance i in the market-hierarchy continuum. X_i is the vector of characteristics of the transaction and of the participating firms (shown in table 4.1), β is the weight attached to each characteristic, and ε_i is a random error term.

Since we only observe the choice of one of three ordered governance modes for each alliance ("FORM$_i$"), we assume that the unobservable variable z_i can be broken up into discrete intervals that "map" into the categories for FORM$_i$.

(2)   If $z_i < \mu_0$ then FORM$_i = 0$

   If $\mu_0 \leq z_i < \mu_1$ then FORM$_i = 1$

   If $z_i \geq \mu_1$ then FORM$_i = 2$

The underlying model consists of the variables (z_i, X_i) given in equation (1). The observed variables are X_i and FORM$_i$, where the observation scheme is given by (2). The objective of the statistical analysis is to estimate β in (1), the parameters that describe the relationship between characteristics of the alliance and participating firms with the position on the market-hierarchy continuum, and how this gets translated into one of the ordered categories of organizational form (FORM$_i$). We can write the probabilities of falling into the various categories of the dependent variable as

(3) $P(\text{FORM}_i = 0 | X_i) = P[\varepsilon_i < (\mu_0 - \beta X_i) | X_i] = \Phi(\mu_0 - \beta X_i)$

   $P(\text{FORM}_i = 1 | X_i) = P[(\mu_0 - \beta X_i) \leq \varepsilon_i < (\mu_1 - \beta X_i) | X_i] =$
   $\Phi(\mu_1 - \beta X_i) - \Phi(\mu_0 - \beta X_i)$

   $P(\text{FORM}_i = 2 | X_i) = P[\varepsilon_i \geq (\mu_1 - \beta X_i) | X_i] = 1 - \Phi(\mu_1 - \beta X_i)$

where $\Phi()$ denotes the cumulative normal distribution function corresponding to the distribution of the random variable ε_i. For the ordered probit model, this is a normal distribution, with the normalization that the variance of $\varepsilon_i = 1$.

Some normalization is also necessary on the (unknown) cut-off points, μ_j. Following common practice, we assume that $\mu_0 = 0$. Then, for the ordered probit model,

(4) $P(\text{FORM}_i = 0 | X_i) = \phi(-\beta X_i)$

   $P(\text{FORM}_i = 1 | X_i) = \phi(\mu_1 - \beta X_i) - \phi(-\beta X_i)$

   $P(\text{FORM}_i = 2 | X_i) = 1 - \phi(\mu_1 - \beta X_i)$

where ϕ is the cumulative distribution for a standardized normal variable.

Empirical results

Estimation results, shown in table 4.3, provide support for most of the transaction cost hypotheses. In model 1, based on the sample of 165 "public company alliances," more hierarchical types of alliance were chosen for design and mixed activity transactions than for alliances governing only production or marketing activities. Thus, as hypothesized, firms choose more hierarchical arrangements in situations where specification of the relevant property rights can be expected to be problematic. Furthermore, the coefficient on "mixed" transactions (2.947) is significantly higher than for design alone (1.225). This parallels Pisano's (1989) findings, that R&D collaborations in the biotechnology industry involving both R&D and other functions were more likely to use equity links than were "pure" R&D agreements.

Table 4.3 Ordered Probit Estimation Results for US-based Alliances

	1	2	3	4
Intercept	−0.127	−0.165	0.574	0.611
	(.373)	(.319)	(.326)	(.349)
Design Transaction	1.225**	1.185**		1.392**
	(.291)	(.280)		(.192)
Mixed Transaction	2.947**	2.966**		2.359**
	(.458)	(.445)		(.160)
Technology Scope	1.225**	1.239**		1.113**
	(.286)	(.257)		(.133)
Geographic Scope	−0.630	−0.679†		−0.481*
	(.405)	(.391)		(.189)
Overlapping Agreements	−0.060	−0.017		0.025
	(.085)	(.080)		(.064)
Number of Partners	n/a	n/a	n/a	0.196*
				(.099)

Table 4.3   (*contd.*)

	1	2	3	4
Biotechnology Dummy	−0.180	−0.231	0.113	−0.264
	(.504)	(.389)	(.330)	(.197)
Info Technology Dummy	−0.244	−0.375	−0.211	−0.088
	(.330)	(.295)	(.252)	(.144)
New Materials Dummy	−0.637	−0.670*	−0.479	−0.344*
	(.325)	(.295)	(.287)	(.174)
Time Trend	0.057	0.042	0.011	0.024
	(.055)	(.046)	(.043)	(.064)
Average Size (Assets)	0.006		0.010	
	(.016)		(.013)	
Asset ratio	−0.194		0.069	
	(.571)		(.394)	
Combined R&D intensity	−1.968		−2.327	
	(4.20)		(3.69)	
R&D Gap	0.051		−1.166	
	(.458)		(1.70)	
Same SIC	0.061		−0.212	
	(.469)		(.324)	
Alliance Experience	−0.004		−0.005	
	(.007)		(.006)	
Log of Likelihood Function	−121.3	−122.3	−172.4	−368.6
Chi–Squared	108.75**	106.67**	10.28	329.26**
Outcomes predicted correctly	73%	73%	37%	73%
Sample Size (n)	165	165	165	507

†$p < 0.10$; *$p < 0.05$; **$p < 0.01$
Standard errors in parentheses

More hierarchical forms were also chosen when multiple products or technologies were involved in an alliance, confirming hypothesis H2, which links this effect to elevated monitoring difficulties (and hence appropriability hazards) associated with the transaction scope.

Overall, model 1 correctly predicts the organizational form of 121 out of the 165 alliances (73.3%). This compares with a random assignment, which would be correct for only 33% of the alliances, or 42% correct if all observations were assigned to the most frequently observed structure, i.e. unilateral contract. Furthermore, as shown in table 4.4, the "hit rate" is significantly higher than would be expected with random predictions in each of the three governance form categories.

Table 4.4   Frequencies of Actual and Predicted Outcomes

Actual Form	*Predicted Form*			*Total*
	0	*1*	*2*	
0	60	6	3	69
1	20	39	1	60
2	5	9	22	36
Total	86	53	26	165

Although it had the expected negative sign, the coefficient on the "overlapping agreements" variable was not statistically different from zero, in contrast to the findings in Gulati's (1995a) study, discussed earlier. A possible explanation for this inconsistency is that the variable used in the present study is an imprecise proxy for ongoing links between the firms: some agreements between relevant firms may not be included in the CATI data, and there is no data available on alliance dissolution or total project value, both of which are relevant to a hostage exchange model of overlapping alliances. Taken together, these limitations suggest that the coefficient on overlapping alliances should be interpreted with caution.

The estimated coefficient on geographic scope is negative, contrary to the hypothesized sign, and is almost significant at the 10% level. Thus, alliances covering worldwide operations, if anything, tend to be *less* hierarchical than those covering only North American operations. This finding should again be interpreted cautiously, however, as we do not have complete information about the age and value of the technology in each alliance, and it is possible that there are systematic but unobserved differences in the characteristics of technology governed in alliances of differing geographic scope. If firms avoid transferring their newest or most valuable technology in situations where monitoring is particularly problematic — e.g. when geographic scope is great — then the observed distribution of alliances in these setting may be skewed toward licensing, which is well-suited for transfer of simpler, more codified technology.[11] More generally, this is a problem of simultaneity in the investment decision: a firm will jointly determine the content and governance of the transaction, i.e. what technology will be shared or transferred, and how that transfer will be organized. Although this study goes further than previous studies in specifying transaction-level variables, it is still not possible to completely control for these effects.

An interesting aspect of the estimation results is that none of the control variables is significant — in contrast to previous studies of the choice between internal organization and joint ventures. Here, we see no significant effect on the form of strategic alliances, of firm size (either average or relative size of the partners), R&D intensity, alliance experience or the industry in which the alliance operates. This result is also supported in models 2 and 3 which show that a model including only the hypothesized variables performs essentially as well as the full model in accurately predicting the alliance form (72.7% of alliances are correctly predicted), while a model including the control variables alone can predict only 37% correctly.

These results emphasize an important finding of the current study: that it is attributes of the transaction, and not firm-level characteristics that determine the type of alliance form chosen. This may also explain the inconsistencies in previous results in the international business literature that are based on firm-level measures, for example with respect to the effect of R&D intensity on governance mode (Gomes-Casseres, 1989).

Estimation of model 4, on the expanded sample of horizontal technology transfer alliances (still involving US-based firms only) produced very similar results to those in model 2, with essentially the same variables. All the coefficients have the same sign as before, with similar levels of significance.[12] However, since this larger sample includes sufficient alliances with more than two partners to allow inclusion of "number of partners" as an independent variable, there is an additional result of interest here: the effect of the number of partners on alliance structure is as hypothesized, suggesting that the increase in anticipated monitoring problems associated with multiple alliance partners induces the partners to choose a more hierarchical alliance structure.

IMPLICATIONS AND CONCLUSIONS

Overall, the results reported here provide strong support for the hypothesis that appropriability hazards are taken into account when firms enter into strategic alliances. When appropriability hazards are severe, because of difficulties in specifying property rights, monitoring contracting partners' activities or enforcing intellectual property rights, more hierarchical types of alliance are chosen. These alliances feature bilateral dependency ("hostage exchange") or equity ties which promote monitoring and incentive alignment. Moreover, in contrast to most related studies in the international business arena, the analysis suggests that the form of an alliance depends primarily on attributes of the transaction itself, rather than on characteristics of the partner firms.

How do these results contribute to the "learning versus leakage" debate raised in the previous chapter? One could argue that the transaction characteristics found to be of importance in alliance mode choice here — the scope and "complexity" (or specification difficulties) of the transaction — are precisely those that are implicated in technology transfer and learning difficulties. As such, the empirical results are consistent with Kogut and Zander's (1993) knowledge-based theory of organizational boundaries. However, the finding that the scope and specification variables are effective in distinguishing between unilateral and bilateral contractual agreements — for which there are no a priori expectations of organizational differences — undermines this explanation. It is nonetheless difficult to untangle the potential effects of "leakage" concerns and "learning" or technology transfer difficulties in the domestic setting (absent more detailed organizational descriptions of various alliance forms) because of the similarity in the variables featured in the two approaches. As demonstrated in the following chapter, pushing the debate forward requires that we move the analysis to the international arena, where variation in the institutional environment adds an additional dimension to governance choice.

FIVE

An Empirical Study of Appropriability Hazards in International Strategic Alliances Stage 2: Cross-National Comparisons

In this chapter I apply the TCE framework to an examination of hybrid organizations that cross international boundaries.[1] While the essential nature of the organizational problems facing firms is the same as in the domestic context, many added complications must be confronted when the focus shifts to the international arena. Additional features of the operating environment include cultural and language differences, government policies that vary across countries (and that are often applied in discriminatory ways against foreign firms), the lack of satisfactory supranational adjudication of disputes, and wide gaps in the relative capabilities of firms.

The framework developed in the previous chapters, in common with most other work in the transaction cost tradition, focused exclusively on the "mechanisms" of governance, whereby economic agents align transactions with governance structures to effect economizing outcomes, taking the institutional environment as given (Williamson, 1996, p. 5). The narrow focus of previous work has sometimes led to criticism that transaction cost economics has developed in relative isolation from the study of the institutional (i.e. legal, social and political) environment. In response, Williamson (1991) introduced a comparative static framework to consider how equilibrium distributions of transactions (and governance structures) change in response to disturbances in the institutional environment. This is done by treating the institutional environment as a set of parameters, changes in which elicit shifts in the comparative costs of governance. Testing the empirical framework developed in Chapter 4, in conjunction with this "shift parameter framework," on a sample of international alliances thus allows an examination of (1) the applicability of the logic developed for domestic governance choices to international organization, and (2) the effects (if any) of national differences in the institutional environment on the choice of governance mode in hybrid organizations.

Although the "shift parameter framework" for analyzing the impact of changes in the institutional environment on governance is conceptually straightforward, empirical tests to date have been elusive. This reflects difficulties in obtaining adequate measures of relevant dimensions of the institutional environment, and in isolating the impact on governance structures. Furthermore, since institutional environments change only slowly and in complex ways, comparative static analysis in a single country setting is problematic. If analysis is shifted to the international arena, however, some of these empirical problems can be mitigated: here we find sufficient heterogeneity in institutional environments to support cross-sectional analysis. In addition, while measurement problems do not disappear, data on several aspects of the institutional environment have been developed and applied in international business research focusing on the institutional determinants of foreign direct investment decisions. These institutional determinants include foreign investment regulations (Contractor, 1990), national cultural differences (Kogut & Singh, 1988; Shane, 1994) as well as aggregated concepts of "political risk" or "investment risk" (e.g., Agarwal & Ramaswami, 1992; Kim & Hwang, 1992).

Stage 2 of the empirical study, described in this chapter, draws on the relevant international business literature, along with a new data source on intellectual property regimes in 110 countries, and applies the shift parameter framework to examine how differences in intellectual property protection and other institutional features affect the governance of technology transfer alliances linking US and non-US firms.

The results of the analysis provide support for the central hypothesis that US companies tend to choose more hierarchical alliances (i.e. equity joint ventures rather than contract-based alliances) when they partner with firms based in countries with weak intellectual property protection. Other national institutional features appear to have few systematic effects on alliance governance structure. Furthermore, the transaction-level variables featured in Stage 1 retain their significance here, with effects paralleling those found in US-only alliances. Thus, a complete understanding of the organization of inter-firm alliances requires that we consider both the institutional environment *and* the mechanisms of governance.

APPROPRIABILITY HAZARDS IN INTERNATIONAL ALLIANCES

When firms attempt to transfer technology across national borders, they face the same "three-stage appropriability problem" as that described earlier for participants in domestic alliances or other hybrid organizations. However, in international arrangements, firms are further challenged by the complex array of regulations and legal institutions found in the various countries where they do business. Ease of enforcement of international contracts depends on the legal regime governing the transaction, notably the efficacy of general contract enforcement. For technology contracts, intellectual property protection is of particular importance: enforcement of intellectual property rights in international alliances is by no means assured, as the strength of protection varies considerably among countries, and specific provisions of intellectual property laws may actually limit protection for some technologies, as discussed below.

National differences in intellectual property protection

Firms transferring technology across national borders must respond to the challenge of varied and imperfect regimes of intellectual property protection. Many countries are signatories to the Paris Convention for the Protection of Industrial Property, which requires that foreign nationals are granted the same intellectual property protection as domestic citizens. However, the convention does not specify what standards of protection should be in place, and the actual level of intellectual property protection varies significantly across countries.

Take, for example, the patent — the most widely used instrument of intellectual property protection for industrial technology. The effective duration[2] of patent protection ranges from 5 years in several Latin American countries to close to 20 years in most European countries (Kondo, 1994). Some technologies may be explicitly excluded from patent protection, such as in India, where product patents are not issued for chemicals, alloys, optical glass, semiconductors or intermetallic compounds (in contrast to most other countries). In addition, some countries require firms to license various patented technologies to local firms (e.g. for drug patents in India and the Philippines), sometimes at very low royalty rates.

Other significant differences occur in the general rules governing the scope of patent protection, including whether a patent holder must work the invention within a specified time limit for it to remain valid, whether the patent application is kept secret until a patent is granted, and whether the patent is awarded to the party who can show that they were the "first to invent' (as in the US) or if it is simply awarded to the "first to file," i.e. apply, for the patent (as in most other countries). These differences in the patent laws, while often arcane, can have a significant impact on the ease of obtaining a patent, and may have the effect of discriminating against foreign firms. For example, according to a 1993 survey on patent-filing costs in 32 countries, the cost of filing in Japan for foreign applicants was alleged to be the highest in the world, due to "translation costs and fees charged by 'benrishi' (Japanese patent attorneys)" (US General Accounting Office, 1993, p. 34).

There is currently a process of international convergence occurring in legal rules governing intellectual property protection. The agreement on Trade Related Aspects of Intellectual

Property Rights (TRIPs), part of the Uruguay Round of GATT negotiations completed in December 1993, calls for the elimination of some of the national differences in patent laws mentioned above. However, the period of phase-in of the relevant changes lasts up to eleven years for the least developed countries, and even then, important exclusions will remain (Chaudhry & Walsh, 1995). Furthermore, enforcement of intellectual property rights relies on the general enforcement powers of the courts — where the judicial system is corrupt, or where property rights and contracts are not respected, firms' ability to contract for the use of valuable intellectual property will be compromised.

Ranking countries by the "strength" of their intellectual property rules is hampered by the multi-dimensionality of protection. However, from the point of view of the intellectual property holder, strong protection is achieved when property rights are easy to establish, are interpreted broadly and are strictly enforced, with substantial penalties for noncompliance.

Implications for governance

Preliminary support for the notion that intellectual property regimes can influence the organization of international technology transfers is provided by Mansfield (1994). Results from this survey of US operations in a limited number of countries suggest that the strength of national intellectual property regimes is positively correlated with aggregate levels of direct foreign investment by US firms. In addition, there is a reported reluctance to transfer advanced technology to unrelated third parties (for example a licensee) in countries with weak intellectual property regimes. According to the vice president for R&D at one chemical company, for example, "We have no situation where we decided not to transfer advanced technology to a country having weak intellectual property laws...[but] we have transferred our advanced technology only to overseas affiliates or joint ventures where we have a substantial equity position and therefore a strong voice in management" (Mansfield, 1994, p. 26).

For US firms partnering with firms in other countries, weak protection of intellectual property in the "foreign" country will tend to raise the cost of relying on contract-based alliances relative to equity joint ventures, so encouraging the use of joint ventures for a wider range of transactions (relative to contracts). This argument is summarized in the following hypothesis:

H6: The degree of hierarchical control in alliances between US and non-US firms is inversely related to the strength of intellectual property protection (i.e. the "appropriability regime") in the "foreign" (non-US) country, ceteris paribus.

The ceteris paribus condition is of critical importance here. If a firm is considering an alliance in an environment of weak protection, it must make two simultaneous decisions: what technology will be shared or transferred and how that transfer will be governed. If a firm responds to weak protection by limiting transactions undertaken to those that are easy to specify and monitor (and hence also somewhat easier to enforce) then this may skew the observed cross-national pattern of alliances. Thus, in empirical analysis, we must simultaneously consider the characteristics of the transaction along with enforcement issues related to the institutional environment.

The relationship between the strength of intellectual property protection and the transaction-level variables implicated in specification and monitoring difficulties, and the resulting simultaneity in the decision regarding the content and governance of inter-firm alliances can be more clearly illustrated using the "shift parameter" framework (Williamson, 1991), an extension of the transaction cost model. Quite simply, the shift parameter framework posits that while the underlying logic informing firms' governance decisions does not vary across nations, differences in institutional environment change the relative costs of alternative governance structures, so that the overall pattern of observed organizational forms may differ across countries. Williamson describes security of property rights (including intellectual property) as one of a range of such shift parameters, and figure 5.1 summarizes the shift parameter logic for the choice between contract-based and equity alliances in the case of a relative weakening in intellectual property protection.[3]

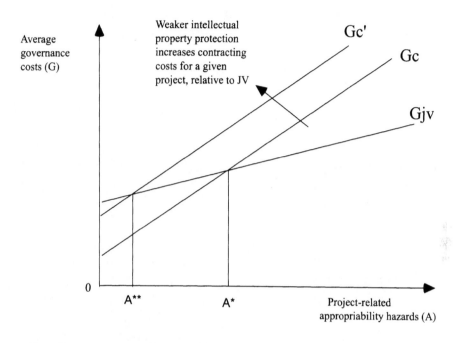

Gc = Governance costs of contractual arrangement
Gjv = Governance costs of equity joint venture

Figure 5.1   The Impact of Intellectual Property Regime on Alliance Form

Note that as intellectual property protection becomes weaker, a narrowing range of transactions are most efficiently governed within a contractual arrangement (from 0-A* with strong protection to 0-A** with weaker protection). Take the example of a US firm with two similar technology transfer projects involving firms based in countries having differing intellectual property protection. If transaction-related appropriability hazards in each case are, say, a little below A*, then we might expect to observe one project governed through a contractual arrangement (in the country with stronger protection), and one organized within an equity joint venture (where protection is weaker). Alternatively, the US firm may choose to use a contractual arrangement in each case, but modify the scope of the project (for example only transferring older or simpler technology) where protection is weak, to bring the transaction-related appropriability hazards below A**.

The implication of this simultaneity in the choice of content and governance of transactions is that we cannot reliably observe the relationship between features of the institutional environment (such as intellectual property protection) and governance choices in inter-firm alliances without also including transaction level variables in the empirical model. We therefore include in the model those transaction characteristics which were earlier found to affect governance choice in domestic alliances.

In the shift parameter framework, the relevant institutional environment impacting optimal governance choice for a given transaction is broadly defined as "the set of fundamental political, social and legal ground rules that establishes the basis for production, exchange and distribution." (Davis & North, 1971, pp. 6–7). Thus, in addition to intellectual property protection, relevant features of the institutional environment may include, for example, cultural differences, government regulation of foreign investment and general political climate. The empirical model described below therefore includes a series of control variables capturing features of the institutional environment that previous research in international business suggests may have an impact on the governance of foreign investments.

EMPIRICAL ANALYSIS

Dependent variable

The new hypothesis links elements of the institutional environment (specifically the host country appropriability regime) to the governance structure of the alliance. Thus, as in Stage 1, the dependent variable (FORM) takes on one of three values:

FORM = 0, for unilateral contractual technology transfer alliances, i.e. for licensing and second sourcing agreements;

FORM = 1, for bilateral contractual technology transfer alliances, i.e. for cross-licensing, mutual second sourcing and technology sharing agreements;

FORM = 2, for equity-based technology transfer alliances, i.e. joint ventures.

Appropriability measure

The country-level variable of central interest is the "national appropriability regime." While there are several previous studies that measure the strength of intellectual property protection in various countries and industries, most suffer from significant shortcomings, particularly in terms of coverage. Some studies (such as Mogee, 1989) focus on only one or two industries, while others (e.g., Mansfield, 1994) cover many industries but include only a few countries. A 1988 study by the US International Trade Commission (1988) surveyed a somewhat broader spectrum of countries, but did not rank countries' intellectual property protection per se; instead US firms were asked to list countries "...in approximate order of importance to you, which you would most like to see adopt fully adequate and effective intellectual property protection" (quoted in Mansfield, 1994, p. 9). This ranking may differ significantly from actual or perceived levels of intellectual property protection.

An alternative measure of intellectual property protection is proposed by Rapp and Rozek (1990). Their index of patent protection ranks the level of patent protection in each nation on a scale of zero to five, based on conformity of the patent laws to the minimum standards proposed by the US Department of Commerce. Unfortunately, although the index is available for 87 countries, there are a several notable exceptions, including Japan, Hong Kong, South Korea and Austria. Since these countries (particularly Japan) account for a significant number of inter-firm agreements with the US their omission severely hampers the utility of Rapp and Rozek's index for this study.[4]

The measure of intellectual property used in the analysis below is one developed by Park and Ginarte (1997). This measure, IPINDEX, is based on an examination of five categories of patent law: extent of coverage, membership in international patent agreements, provisions for loss of protection,[5] enforcement mechanisms and duration of protection.[6] The index shares some of the limitations of previous intellectual property measures, particularly with respect to the narrow focus on patents rather than on alternative forms of protection (such as copyright or trade secret law). However, the inclusion of enforcement issues in the index — i.e. the availability of preliminary injunctions, contributory infringement pleadings and burden-of-proof reversals — mitigates an important shortcoming of alternative measures. In addition, IPINDEX is available for a broader range of countries (110 in all) yielding a larger sample of alliances for which complete data are available.[7]

Control variables

In addition to the measures of appropriability regime, several other country-level variables are included in the empirical model to address alternative explanations proposed in previous research. These control variables are as follows:

Cultural distance.   Kogut and Singh (1988) argue that cultural distance increases the cost of acquisitions relative to greenfield investment or joint ventures for foreign investors, because of difficulties in integrating existing foreign management. This argument would also suggest higher costs for joint ventures relative to more arms-length contracts as cultural distance increases management integration costs. However, cultural distance is also likely to increase contracting costs related to monitoring and enforcement (due to a lack of familiarity with relevant aspects of the legal system, for example), Thus, as illustrated in figure 5.2, the net effect on the threshold level delimiting the least-cost governance mode is ambiguous and the impact of cultural distance on the choice between equity joint ventures and contract-based alliances is indeterminate.

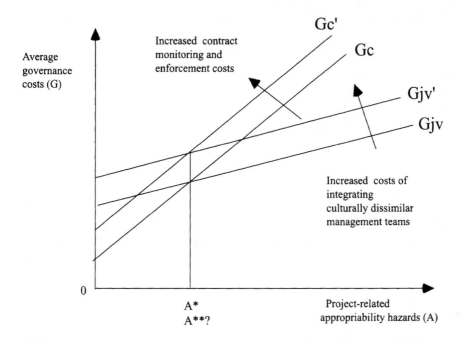

Figure 5.2 The Impact of "Cultural Distance" on Alliance Form

To assess the applicability of their argument to this particular empirical sample, Kogut and Singh's (1988) composite index of "cultural distance," between the US and the home country of the "foreign" partner firm, is included in the model. Based on Hofstede's (1980) "dimensions of culture," cultural distance (CULDISTj) is measured as the deviation across each of the four dimensions (power distance, uncertainty avoidance, individualism and masculinity), corrected for variance differences among the dimensions.[8]

Societal Trust. Shane (1994) suggests that "societal trust" may have an impact on the organization of US firms' overseas operations: in "high trust" cultures, less monitoring is necessary to deter opportunistic behavior, and therefore contracting is feasible for a wider range of transactions, relative to more hierarchical modes. While Shane's analysis is based only on aggregate licensing and foreign direct investment flows from the US to the countries in the study, the argument is nonetheless applicable here, where we would expect an increase in societal trust to be related to an increased use of contractual arrangements in alliances, relative to equity joint ventures.

Absent a definitive measure for societal trust, the proxy most commonly used in previous work is also adopted here — one based on Hofstede's (1980) "power distance" scale. This scale actually represents the extent to which members of a society expect power to be distributed equally within organizations and institutions, but power distant societies also tend to exhibit less interpersonal trust and a greater need for external controls on the behavior of individuals. Therefore we use $TRUST_j$, the negative of power distance, as the proxy for the level of societal trust in the non-US partner's home country j.[9]

Education.   Education levels in the "host" country are frequently adopted as control variables in cross-national studies of foreign entry governance mode (e.g., Davidson & McFetridge, 1985). The rationale relies on Cohen & Levinthal's (1990, p. 128) notion of "absorptive capacity," that "the ability to evaluate and utilize outside knowledge is largely a function of prior related knowledge." In a survey of the impact of inward technology transfer on national competitiveness, Mowery and Oxley (1995) concluded that those countries with high "national absorptive capacity," based on the development of a well-educated and technically trained workforce, were able to benefit most from inward technology transfer. It is therefore a plausible implication of a knowledge-based view of alliances that countries with more highly-educated populations are better able to absorb technical information and capabilities through an arms-length arrangement: in this case, we expect that the cost of technology transfer through arms-length modes will be reduced, relative to the cost of transfer within a joint venture. From a transaction cost perspective, in the choice between contractual forms and equity joint ventures, the inference is that a greater level of demonstration, training, etc., will be necessary when partner capabilities diverge, and since these activities pose contracting hazards, the relative costs of contractual arrangements will increase.

Two measures of education level are adopted in the study to control for the potential impact of non-US firms' capabilities on alliance form. The first measure, EDUCPER$_{jt}$, is the secondary school enrollment rate, as a percentage of population in the appropriate age group. The limitation of this measure is that contemporaneous levels of secondary school enrollment may not accurately reflect the education level of the adult labor force available to alliance participants. An additional measure is therefore considered: EDUCYRS$_{jt}$, the average years of higher schooling (i.e. beyond secondary school) in the total population over age 25 (Barro & Lee, 1993). Since this latter data is available only quinquennially, values for interim years are estimated using linear interpolation.

Investment regulations.   Governments may directly intervene in foreign firms' investment decisions. Therefore, following Contractor (1990), a composite measure of performance requirements (INVESTREG$_j$), derived from the 1982 Benchmark Survey of the US Department of Commerce (1985), is included as a proxy for investment regulations imposed on US-owned joint ventures in country j.[10] This measure is based on the sum of the proportion of all US affiliates in a nation that are subject to an export minimum, an import limit and/or a local content minimum.[11]

Political risk.   "Political risk," broadly defined, may be a significant concern for foreign investors, and there is some evidence that political instability deters foreign direct investment (Kobrin, 1976; Root & Ahmed, 1978). Alliance governance costs may also be affected: for example, political upheaval has historically been associated with increased risk of government expropriation of foreign-held assets in many countries, potentially raising the cost of equity joint ventures relative to contractual alliances with local firms. However, the security of contracts with local firms is also likely to be negatively affected by increased political risk (due to lack of confidence in the enforcement powers of the courts). Thus, the impact of political risk on the organization of inter-firm alliances is unclear.[12] Measures of political risk are nonetheless included as control variables.

The multidimensionality of political risk and the scarcity of adequate time-series measures pose challenges in variable construction. One available measure, the Euromoney measure of country risk, is based on the rating of a nation's debt in the international financial markets. This measure thus combines elements of political and economic risk.[13] While the measure is available for each sample year, the methodology used in constructing the index changed significantly several times during the period, making year-to-year comparisons problematic. Two alternative measures based on this index are therefore adopted: $POLITIC_j$ is the Euromoney index for 1985 for each of the countries in the sample. This index, on a scale of 0 to 100, ranges in our sample from 11.6 (for Chile) to 100 (for Japan, Australia, Canada and several European countries), with higher levels indicating greater political stability and lower country risk. $POLRANK_{jt}$ is the ordinal ranking of each country based on the index, in each of the sample years.

Market size.   Measures of market size and growth are frequently included in empirical studies of foreign market entry mode, although with inconsistent results.[14] Although the impact of market size and growth on alliance structure is ambiguous, both are included as control variables. The measure of market size is the natural log of real GDP (in 1985 US dollars) for the year of establishment of the alliance, and market growth rate is proxied by average annual growth in GNP/capita. Data for each of these measures, $LGDP_{jt}$ and $GROWTH_{jt}$, come from the Penn World Tables (Summers & Heston, 1991).

Previous alliance structure.   Evolutionary economists argue that "history matters" since firms develop routines that shape their strategic and organizational choices (Nelson & Winter, 1982). If this is the case, then the likelihood of a particular alliance being organized as an equity joint venture will depend, in part, on the partners' experience, and their over-all propensity to use this type of alliance structure. Further-more, there may be important cross-national differences in the types of alliances favored by firms. For each partner firm in alliance i, the percentage of all previous alliances that were organized as an equity joint venture is therefore calcu-lated and the variable $JVPERCENT_i$ is the average of these measures for the two alliance partners. To ensure that this variable does not simply capture general alliance experience (since $JVPERCENT_i$ is by definition zero for all firms with no previous alliances) $EXPERIENCE_i$, the average of a simple count of previous alliances for the two partners in alliance i, is also included.

Transaction characteristics, etc. To address the simultaneity issues raised earlier, and to facilitate comparison with the results from the Stage 1 analysis of US alliances, the following transaction and relational variables are also included (with de-finitions as before): Transaction type, technology scope, and overlapping agreements. Sector controls (biotechnology, new materials and information technology) are also included.

Sample and Descriptive Statistics

The initial sample drawn from the CATI data comprised all bilateral technology transfer alliances in the database that were established between 1980–89, involved one US-based firm allied with a firm based in another country and whose activities were centered in one of the technologies designated by the CATI compilers as a "core" technology, i.e. biotechno-logy, information technology or new materials. This yielded a sample of 773 alliances from 34 countries. Focusing on the "core technologies" (which together comprise approximately

65% of the total alliances documented in the CATI database) mitigates some of the under-reporting and biases mentioned earlier, since the secondary sources used in compilation of the CATI data are concentrated in these three sectors. In addition, as neither firm-level nor industry-level data are available for firms in the large number of countries in the analysis, reducing the number of industries considered has the added advantage of removing some potential variation in industry-level effects while still maintaining an adequate sample size.

Elimination of alliances for which some of the country data was unavailable further reduced the sample to 727 alliances in 27 countries. Of these, 343 are unilateral contract-based alliances, i.e. technology licenses and second sourcing agreements and 170 are bilateral contracts (cross-license agreements, mutual second sourcing and technology sharing agreements). The remaining 214 alliances are organized as equity joint ventures and all involve product design and/or manufacture and marketing. Thus, in contrast to the US-only agreements, which were very evenly distributed across the three governance categories, here we see a somewhat bi-modal distribution. Unilateral contracts account for over 40% of the agreements, and approximately 35% are equity joint ventures. Less than 25% of agreements fall in the middle category of bilateral contracts. This may suggest that the use of hostage exchanges in the context of cross-national contracts is less effective than in contracts between firms of the same nationality.

The country distribution of the sample of alliances, shown in table 5.1, reveals some noteworthy characteristics, most particularly the dominance of Japanese and European companies in the sample. This distribution actually mirrors that in the broader CATI data quite closely. Among a total of over 1800 inter-firm alliances (of many types) linking US and overseas firms, approximately 50% are with European firms, 40% with Japanese firms and all other countries account for the remainder, approximately 10% (Duysters & Hagedoorn, 1996). The concentration of alliances within the "triad" of North America, Europe and Japan, which has also been documented elsewhere (e.g., Hergert & Morris, 1988), also is broadly consistent with the global pattern of economic activity (based on 1985 GNP data).

Table 5.1   Distribution of Alliances Across Countries

Country	No. of Alliances
Australia	7
Austria	2
Belgium	7
Brazil	1
Canada	19
Chile	1
Denmark	4
Finland	3
France	47
Germany	57
Hong Kong	1
India	4
Ireland	1
Israel	6
Italy	52
Japan	325
Mexico	1
Netherlands	54
New Zealand	1
Norway	4
Singapore	1
Spain	5
Sweden	23
Switzerland	20
Thailand	1
United Kingdom	82
Venezuela	2

Table 5.2 presents descriptive statistics and table 5.3 shows the correlation matrix for the independent variables. Many of

Table 5.2 Descriptive Statistics for Independent Variables, Stage 2

	Variable	Description	Mean (Std. Dev.)	Range	Expected Sign
HYPOTHESIS VARIABLES	SCOPE	Multiple technologies involved in project	0.429 (0.50)	0 or 1	+
	DESIGN	Design or development only	0.054 (0.23)	0 or 1	+
	MIXED	Mixed activities (design & production)	0.209 (0.41)	0 or 1	+
	IPINDEX	Patent strength indicator	3.84 (0.42)	0.75 to 4.33	−
CONTROL VARIABLES Institutional environment	CULDIST	Cultural distance, based on Hofstede	1.662 (0.99)	0.02 to 4.01	?
	TRUST	Negative of Hofstede "Power Distance" scale	−48.24 (11.29)	−11.0 to −81.0	−
	EDUCPER	Secondary school enrollment rate	0.909 (0.10)	0.30 to 1.09	−
	EDUCYRS	Ave. years of higher schooling in adult population	0.405 (0.11)	0.09 to 0.67	−
	INVESTREG	FDI performance requirements (1982)	0.011 (0.02)	0.00 to 0.31	−

	POLRISK	Euromoney's country risk measure (1985)	96.70 (9.01)	11.6 to 100	?
	POLRANK	Rank in Euromoney's country risk rating	4.923 (7.00)	1 to 59	?
	LGDP	Natural Log of Real GDP (in 1985 US dollars)	20.37 (0.92)	16.74 to 21.25	?
	GROWTH	Growth in GNP/Capita	2.759 (0.87)	−1.3 to 5.9	?
Firm history	OVERLAP	No. of previous alliances linking current partners	0.607 (1.24)	0 to 9	−
	EXPERIENCE	Average of prev. alliance experience for 2 partners	26.23 (30.64)	0 to 187	?
	JVPERCENT	Proportion of previous alliances organized as JVs	0.185 (0.16)	0 to 1	+
Sector controls	BIOTECH	Alliance activities in biotech sector	0.208 (0.41)	0 or 1	?
	MATERIALS	Alliance activities in new materials sector	0.249 (0.39)	0 or 1	?

Table 5.3 Correlation Matrix for Independent Variables, Stage 2

	1	2	3	4	5	6	7	8	9	10	11	12	13	14	15
1. SCOPE	1.00														
2. DESIGN	0.003	1.00													
3. MIXED	0.242	-0.124	1.00												
4. IPINDEX	0.088	0.059	-0.027	1.00											
5. CULDIST	-0.014	0.013	-0.031	0.046	1.00										
6. TRUST	-0.011	0.025	0.025	0.128	-0.605	1.00									
7. EDUCPER	0.019	0.043	-0.088	0.720	0.344	0.123	1.00								
8. EDUCYRS	-0.048	0.039	-0.075	0.153	0.613	-0.056	0.542	1.00							
9. INVESTREG	-0.041	-0.048	0.002	-0.661	0.110	-0.359	-0.382	-0.154	1.00						
10. POLRISK	0.021	0.044	-0.114	0.622	0.058	0.392	0.724	0.549	-0.535	1.00					
11. POLRANK	-0.028	-0.056	0.098	-0.466	-0.166	-0.171	-0.580	-0.520	0.385	-0.868	1.00				
12. LGDP	0.017	0.022	-0.007	0.617	-0.125	0.333	0.110	0.271	0.005	0.211	-0.425	1.00			
13. GROWTH	0.020	0.026	-0.047	0.174	0.594	-0.340	0.211	0.282	-0.101	0.365	-0.473	0.734	1.00		
14. OVERLAP	0.125	0.047	-0.034	0.098	0.113	-0.066	0.056	0.059	-0.057	0.040	-0.078	0.109	0.109	1.00	
15. EXPERIENCE	0.104	0.038	0.006	0.157	0.059	-0.056	0.054	0.047	-0.077	-0.001	0.009	0.113	0.065	0.443	1.00
16. JVPERCENT	0.103	0.030	0.134	0.011	0.086	-0.127	0.036	0.007	0.049	-0.016	-0.049	0.065	0.035	0.052	0.070

the country-level variables are correlated, as one would expect. For example the measure of intellectual property protection (IPINDEX) is positively correlated with a measure of educational attainment (EDUCPER) and market size (LGDP), negatively related to government-imposed performance requirements (INVESTREG) and country risk (POLRANK). These associations are to be expected, and are consistent with the general observation that economic development provides motivation for the development of institutions to provide effective intellectual property protection (Park & Ginarte, 1997; Rapp & Rozek, 1990).

Results and discussion

The model was first estimated using an ordered probit model, as described in the previous chapter, where the dependent variable (FORM) can take on one of three ordered categories (0 = unilateral contract, 1 = bilateral contract and 2 = equity joint venture). However, the model was unable to differentiate among the three governance forms: Instead, the predicted value of the dependent variable was always either 0 or 2, as shown in table 5.4.[15]

Table 5.4   Governance Form Predictions of Ordered Probit Model

| Actual Form | Predicted Form | | | |
	0	1	2	Total
0	314	0	29	343
1	135	0	35	170
2	41	0	173	214
Total	490	0	237	727

Notice that the model correctly predicts the governance form for unilateral contracts (FORM = 0) in 90% of the cases, and 80% for joint ventures (FORM = 2), significantly exceeding the number of correct predictions that would be expected from a random process. Bilateral contracts (FORM = 1) are thrown in with unilateral contracts, 80% of the time. This provides support for the suggestion made earlier, that hostage exchanges in cross-national contracts are less effective than in contracts between firms of the same nationality and that firms effectively choose between just two discrete structural alternatives for agreements with firms from other nations — i.e., contracts and equity joint ventures. The models were therefore re-estimated as binomial logit models,[16] with equity as the dependent variable, where:

EQUITY = 0, for unilateral and bilateral contractual agreements, i.e. licensing contracts, technology sharing and second sourcing agreements (previously FORM = 0 and FORM = 1)

EQUITY = 1, for equity joint ventures (previously FORM = 2)

Simple appropriability model.   Estimation results for a "simple" appropriability model of alliance governance are shown in table 5.5, and provide support for the transaction cost hypotheses. In model 5, the coefficient on IPINDEX (−0.826), the indicator of patent strength, or appropriability regime, is negative, as hypothesized, and significant at the 1% level. This suggests that US firms are more likely to organize an alliance as an equity joint venture when the partner is from a country where intellectual property protection is weak (all else being equal).

The transaction level variables in these models are also highly significant and are consistent with results found in the analysis of alliances involving US-based firms (Stage 1). Design and mixed activities are more likely to be organized within equity joint ventures than are pure production or marketing activities, suggesting that specification difficulties lead to the adoption of the joint venture structure. The coefficient on mixed transactions (4.973 in model 5) is also significantly larger than that for design (3.259), as before. The predicted impact of monitoring difficulties on alliance structure is also observed, as wider technology scope is associated with equity arrangements, with a positive and significant coefficient. These results confirm the similarities in the essential organizational problems facing firms in the domestic and international settings.

Table 5.5 Estimation Results: Simple Appropriability Model

	5	6	7	8
INTERCEPT	−0.155	0.154	−0.565	−0.077
	(.965)	(1.19)	(1.05)	(1.27)
SCOPE	1.305**	1.322**	1.367**	1.404**
	(.286)	(.288)	(.292)	(.296)
DESIGN	3.259**	3.268**	3.261**	3.275**
	(.409)	(.410)	(.409)	(.410)
MIXED	4.973**	4.991**	5.008**	5.046**
	(.371)	(.372)	(.377)	(.380)
IPINDEX	−0.826**	−1.048*	−0.782**	−1.122*
	(.254)	(.459)	(.260)	(.259)
BIOTECH	−0.144	−0.127	−0.191	−0.153
	(.409)	(.412)	(.408)	(.411)
MATERIALS	1.121**	1.091**	1.120**	1.095**
	(.315)	(.317)	(.318)	(.321)
JAPAN	n/a	0.588	n/a	0.898
		(.879)		(.887)
EUROPE	n/a	0.552	n/a	0.750
		(.854)		(.856)
ASIANIC	n/a	1.554	n/a	1.715
		(1.508)		(1.52)
YR82–83	n/a	n/a	0.197	0.193
			(.441)	(.446)
YR84–85	n/a	n/a	−0.287	−0.297
			(.468)	(.471)
YR86–87	n/a	n/a	0.313	0.331
			(.424)	(.436)
YR88–89	n/a	n/a	0.671	0.744
			(.428)	(.440)
Log Likelihood	−204.01	−203.40	−201.30	−200.34
Chi-Squared	473.12**	474.34**	478.53**	480.46**
"Hit Rate"	90.9%	90.9%	90.6%	90.8%
Sample Size (n)	727	727	727	727

*$p < 0.05$; **$p < 0.01$
Standard errors in parentheses

Adding dummy variables for the major geographic areas (model 6) does not materially change these results (except that the significance of the IPINDEX is lowered slightly, to 2%) and none of the area dummies are significant. Furthermore, estimating the model on a sample with all Japanese alliances removed produced essentially identical results. Nor does adding dummy variables for the establishment year of the alliance change the results (models 7 & 8).[17] A Chi-squared test reveals that the area and year controls do not collectively add to the explanatory power of the model. The industry dummy for alliances involved in the new materials sector is significant and positive in each case, however, suggesting that both biotechnology and information technology alliances are more likely to be organized as contract-based alliances than are alliances in the new materials sector.

The overall predictive power of the appropriability model is excellent: the "correct" prediction regarding governance mode is made for over 90% of the agreements in the sample in each case, significantly better than a random assignment (58% correct) or the simple assignment of all predicted outcomes to the contractual category (70% correct).

Coefficients from a logit estimation cannot be directly interpreted in terms of the effect on the dependent variable, since the logit is not a linear form. The effect of a change in an independent variable on the probability of an alliance having an equity joint venture structure can nonetheless be calculated, for a given starting level of that variable and values of other variables in the model. For a change in a given country-level variable, from x_{jt} to x'_{jt}, this is calculated as:

$$\frac{\exp\{\beta(X_i, X_{jt})\}}{[1 + \exp\{\beta(X_i, X_{jt})\}]} - \frac{\exp\{\beta(X_i, X'_{jt})\}}{[1 + \exp\{\beta(X_i, X'_{jt})\}]}$$

where X_i is the vector of alliance-specific independent variables, X_{jt} and X'_{jt} are vectors of country-level independent variables, and X_{jt} and X'_{jt} differ only with respect to the change in the variable under investigation from x_{jt} to x'_{jt}.

The results of such calculations based on the estimations in model 5 provide some interesting insights into alliance partners' choice of organizational form: changes in the scope and type of activities in an alliance have a large impact on the probability that an alliance will be organized as an equity joint venture. For example, with all other variables evaluated at their means, moving from an alliance covering only a single technology to one involving multiple technologies increases the probability of an equity joint venture structure from 6.2% to 19.6%. Comparing an alliance engaging in design activities to one involving only production and marketing activities, we see an increase in the probability of equity sharing from 3.3% to 47%; and with a mixture of production and design activities, this probability increases to 83%.

What about the impact of intellectual property protection? For small increases in the patent strength indicator (e.g. from the mean to one standard deviation higher), the reduction in probability of a joint venture structure is quite modest — under 4% in each of the models. However, if we look at the effect of moving an alliance, for example, from the United Kingdom (with an IPINDEX value of 3.67) to India (with a value of 1.33), the probability of a joint venture structure goes from 22% to 62%. Together, these results suggest that the activities involved in an alliance are the primary drivers of alliance structure choice, but that the strength of intellectual property protection is also a significant factor.

Appropriability model with other institutional environment controls. Table 5.6 reports results for models that include control variables designed to capture the effects of other national differences in institutional environment. Since there are two alternative measures for each of "foreign" country education level and political risk, models 9–12 were estimated with different combinations of these variables along with the other hypothesis and control variables. The coefficients on the transaction level variables and IPINDEX are comparable in magnitude (with the latter at slightly lower levels of significance) to those in the "simple" appropriability models in table 5.5.

Table 5.6   Estimation Results with Additional Control Variables

	9	10	11	12
INTERCEPT	2.109	2.633	0.619	1.474
	(4.09)	(4.10)	(4.70)	(4.34)
SCOPE	1.258**	1.262**	1.262**	1.267**
	(.298)	(.298)	(.299)	(.298)
DESIGN	3.366**	3.357**	3.380**	3.366**
	(.422)	(.422)	(.423)	(.422)
MIXED	5.003**	4.995**	5.004**	4.993**
	(.380)	(.379)	(.380)	(.379)
IPINDEX	−0.955*	−0.875†	−0.948*	−0.899*
	(.441)	(.483)	(.436)	(0.412)
CULDIST	0.127	0.177	0.145	−0.184
	(.215)	(.221)	(.211)	(.220)
TRUST	−0.007	−0.006	−0.008	−0.006
	(.018)	(.018)	(.018)	(.019)
EDUCPER	0.306	n/a	0.843	n/a
	(2.24)		(1.89)	
EDUCYRS	n/a	−0.053	n/a	−0.108
		(1.19)		(1.096)
INVESTREG	−2.608	−1.915	−1.645	−2.025
	(8.06)	(7.95)	(7.40)	(7.71)
POLRISK	−0.017	−0.007	n/a	n/a
	(.027)	(.025)		
POLRANK	n/a	n/a	0.016	0.011
			(.028)	(.026)
LGDP	−0.127	−0.139	−0.108	−0.113
	(.237)	(.240)	(.246)	(.250)
GROWTH	0.003	−0.032	−0.015	−0.028
	(.257)	(.257)	(.249)	(.251)
OVERLAP	−0.105	−0.107	−0.103	−0.105
	(.125)	(.124)	(.125)	(.125)
EXPERIENCE	0.005	0.005	0.005	0.005
	(.005)	(.005)	(.005)	(.005)
JVPERCENT	2.557**	2.547**	2.567**	2.556**
	(.837)	(.838)	(.837)	(.838)
Log Likelihood	−196.68	−196.85	−196.70	−196.79
Chi-Squared	487.77	487.44	487.74	487.55
"Hit Rate"	91.2%	91.2%	91.2%	91.2%
Sample Size (n)	727	727	727	727

†$p < 0.10$; *$p < 0.05$; **$p < 0.01$
Standard errors in parentheses

None of the control variables capturing other aspects of the institutional environment are significant in these models. For example, the estimated coefficient on CULDIST (cultural distance) is positive, but insignificant at the 10% level. This is consistent with the prediction that the impact of cultural distance on the choice between contract-based alliances and equity joint ventures is ambiguous.

The sign of the coefficient on TRUST is negative, consistent with Shane's (1994) findings on the choice between foreign direct investment and licensing, but, once again, the effect is not statistically significant. A possible explanation is related to the focus here on border-crossing inter-firm alliances. As noted by Shane, it is not clear that business people in high trust cultures will transfer this trust to people from *other* cultures — an implicit assumption made when applying these concepts to cross-national alliance activity. Indeed, citing Japan as the archetype of a high-trust culture, Shane argues that entrepreneurs there " ... see natives as in-group members and foreigners as out-group members. Entrepreneurs in these societies stress the differences between foreigners and natives and may not trust foreigners" (p. 630). This effect could make contractual relationships with US firms particularly problematic and so confound any effect of higher societal trust on the choice between equity joint ventures and contract-based alliances.

The presence of government-imposed performance requirements also does not apparently discourage the use of equity joint ventures relative to contract-based forms. INVESTREG has a negative coefficient as expected, but is statistically insignificant. Thus, while government-imposed requirements on US affiliates have a significant impact on the choice between majority- and minority-owned ventures (Contractor, 1990), this effect does not appear to extend to the choice between equity joint ventures and contractual alliances. Nor do the measures of education, political and country risk or market size and growth appear to capture anything of significance to US firms choosing between contract-based alliances and equity joint ventures.

Firm history and previous alliance activity.   The relational variables included in the model yield some interesting additional results. First, as in the Stage 1 analysis, the number of previous alliances between partner firms (OVERLAP) does not have a significant effect on alliance structure in this sample, although the same caveats regarding interpretation of this result apply.

Firm history does appear to matter, however, in the choice of alliance structure. While general alliance experience does not have a significant effect, a joint venture structure is more likely to be chosen by firms who have previously favored this form of alliance: the probability that an alliance is organized as a joint venture is positively and significantly related (at the 1% level) to the proportion of each partner firm's previous alliances that were also joint ventures. This observation suggests a role for firm history in governance choice, and highlights the potential importance of organizational routines in shaping and limiting firms' organizational choices (Nelson & Winter, 1982), thereby creating organizational inertia or "strategic momentum" (Amburgey & Miner, 1992; Miller & Friesen, 1980). Alternatively, the result may simply reflect unobserved heterogeneity in the types of projects undertaken by firms in the sample. In any case, firm history does not override transaction cost considerations, suggesting that a useful approach to governance questions is to maintain the transaction as the unit of analysis, but also to consider the potential impact of firm history and interdependencies across transactions.

IMPLICATIONS AND CONCLUSIONS

Overall, the results of this empirical test of Williamson's (1991) "shift parameter framework" provides strong support for the central transaction cost hypotheses. Appropriability hazards are an important factor in US firms' choice of governance mode when they enter into cooperative agreements with foreign firms, and these effects operate at two levels — at the transaction level and at the institutional environment level. The results thus support the contention that "the institutional environment (laws, polity, etc.) and the institutions of governance (markets, hierarchies, etc.) matter a lot and in ways that are pertinent to industrial organization and much else, such as...business strategy [and] multinational business..." (Williamson, 1996, p. 4).

This empirical analysis of course has limitations. Most obviously, some of the country-level measures adopted, although the best available, are rough proxies for the underlying phenomena. This prompts cautious interpretation of the results. Nonetheless, the significance of the appropriability regime effect on alliance form choice, coupled with the lack of significance of other institutional variables does suggest that a complete explanation of organizational choice must include transaction cost arguments. The strength of intellectual property protection is central to a theory of alliance structure based on "leakage" concerns, but plays no part in a "pure" knowledge-based theory of firm boundaries. Rather, from this viewpoint, one would expect national education levels to be significant predictors of international variation in observed forms. Thus, the findings in this study fail to support knowledge-based theories of organizational form that do not acknowledge the opportunism-mitigating characteristics of organizations.

Another potential limitation of the study is that the countries represented in the sample are mainly from within the "triad" of the US, Europe and Japan. However, as noted earlier, this is quite representative of the global pattern of alliance and economic activity. Indeed, the infrequency of alliances between firms from the triad countries and firms in developing countries almost certainly reflects concerns regarding leakage of intellectual property, along with the obvious scarcity of valuable resources and capabilities offered by developing country firms. Only where appropriability risks are offset by huge anticipated gains from rapid market development (such as in China in recent years) are we likely to see significant alliance activity.

SIX

Conclusions and Suggestions for Future Research

The dramatic growth in the founding of joint ventures and other cooperative agreements among international firms over the past fifteen years has spawned a large and diverse literature seeking to understand the phenomenon. This literature has provided important insight into the issues facing managers of international "hybrids," but it has also favored rich description over theoretical rigor, and focused on the idiosyncrasies of international operations rather than on the core organizational issues that are common to managers of both domestic and multinational firms. The implications of this trend are clearly understood by Donald Lessard, past president of the Academy of International Business:

If IB [International Business] cuts itself off from other disciplines and fields of study in management, it will become sterile and virtually ensure that others will not pay attention to it . . . I believe that we have little choice but to try to maintain close linkages with the underlying disciplines and functions, and to have a coherent focus of our own (Lessard, 1995, p. 3).

The work in this study suggests that such linkages, between international business research and underlying disciplines, can indeed be fruitful. Building on recent theoretical developments in transaction cost economics I systematically examined factors influencing the formation of international strategic alliances and undertook a large-scale empirical study of the influence of appropriability hazards and intellectual property protection on the structure of alliances. By developing a transaction cost treatment of international hybrid arrangements, I demonstrated that apparently idiosyncratic features of international hybrids are indeed susceptible to analysis through the albeit narrow lens of transaction cost economics. Furthermore, the similarity of the empirical results from analysis of alliances involving US firms only with those from analysis of "border-crossing" alliances provides compelling evidence that the essential organizational problems are similar in each case.

The above should not be interpreted as suggesting that opportunities for learning arise only from the application of disciplinary insights to international business, however. The variety of institutional environments facing firms in the international arena challenge the boundaries of theoretical and empirical development in disciplines such as transaction cost economics. Application of transaction cost economics to issues of international organization highlights the implications of these institutional differences on firms' organizational choices — an area that has been underdeveloped in previous work in the discipline. Closer examination of these issues as they relate to the formation of international hybrids brings operational content to the "shift parameter framework," a recent extension of the transaction cost approach (Williamson, 1991). Because international strategic alliances are frequently formed to govern the transfer of technology, empirical examination of these "new" forms of organization also increases our understanding of the role of appropriability hazards in governance.

The key findings of the 2-part empirical study of appropriability hazards in international strategic alliances are as follows: First, as hypothesized, appropriability hazards are a significant predictor of organizational form in inter-firm alliances. More hierarchical alliance modes are associated with transaction characteristics that imply difficulties in property rights specification, monitoring or enforcement. Second, in "domestic" (US-only) alliances, three distinct governance modes in the "market-hierarchy continuum" of hybrid organizations can be distinguished empirically: unilateral contracts, bilateral contracts, and equity joint ventures. Furthermore, in contrast to the findings of many previous international business studies, firm-level characteristics (such as size, R&D spending and alliance experience) are not found to be significant predictors of governance form. This suggests that, at least for this narrow range of organizational choices, the relevant level of analysis is indeed the transaction, and not the firm, as implicitly assumed in most current theories and empirical analyses in international business.

In the analysis of alliances linking US and non-US firms, similar transaction-level effects are observed, but in this arena, the governance differences of the two contractual alliance forms are not distinguishable in the empirical results. This may be interpreted to suggest that hostage exchanges in cross-national contracts are less effective than in contracts between firms of the same nationality — perhaps because reputation effects are less reliable. As a result, firms essentially choose between just two discrete structural alternatives for agreements with firms from other nations — i.e. contracts and joint ventures. Although transaction-level characteristics are the primary drivers of governance choice in international alliances, intellectual property protection is also a significant factor. Thus, a complete understanding of the organization of inter-firm alliances requires that we consider both the institutional environment *and* the mechanisms of governance.

The theoretical and empirical results also serve to clarify a recent debate about the relative importance of leakage hazards in alliances and their impact on the ability of firms to learn from alliance partners. In addition to suggestions that opportunism is unnecessary to explain the boundaries of the firm (Conner & Prahalad, 1996; Kogut & Zander, 1992), some authors have suggested that steps taken to mitigate opportunism and associated hazards such as technology leakage can actually hamper efforts to learn in alliances. For example, Zajac and Olsen (1993, p. 132 & p. 143) suggest that, "... the pursuit of greater joint value [in inter-firm arrangements] requires the use of governance structures that are *less* efficient from a transaction cost perspective... strategic and learning gains often increase transaction value while simultaneously increasing transaction costs." The arguments and empirical analysis presented here suggest, however, that knowledge-based theories of the firm provide only partial explanations of governance choice in alliances, and cannot account for the observed impact of intellectual property protection on international alliance structures. Furthermore, transaction cost reasoning suggests that efficient governance structures for inter-firm cooperation are those that embody "credible commitments" by partner firms to engage in mutually beneficial behavior, for example through the sharing of equity in a joint venture. These structures simultaneously reduce the risk of leakage of valuable technology while enhancing opportunities for learning among alliance partners.

SUGGESTIONS FOR FUTURE RESEARCH

There are many avenues for future research — both theoretical and empirical — that are suggested by the results of this study. Below, I focus on extensions of the empirical analysis and a longer-term research agenda, synthesizing insights from transaction cost economics with those from the "resource-based view" to explore "learning and leakage" in international alliances

Empirical extensions and longitudinal studies

One of the major limitations of the empirical analysis reported here, is the lack of data on specific technologies involved in the sample alliances. As a result, it is not possible to determine when and if simultaneity issues are responsible for some of the observed results (e.g. for the effect of geographic scope on governance choice), as discussed in Chapters 4 and 5. To get around this problem, we would like to have significant additional data. This would include information on the type of technology in an alliance, in terms of its value and level of advancement relative to the "state of the art" (which together determine the upper bound on the losses associated with appropriability hazards in the relationship). We would also like to have measures of the "tacitness" of know-how involved in technology transfers, and the efficacy of intellectual property protection available (which are important determinants of the level of appropriability hazards). This type of micro-analytic data is not obtainable from existing large-scale data sets, and so a survey-based approach is called for.

Even more ambitious extensions to the empirical research would include an empirical investigation of the interactions between different types of contracting hazards in alliances — e.g., asset specificity and appropriability hazards — and how mitigation of these hazards is achieved in environments where rapid "real-time response" is necessary. The data requirements and complexities of such undertakings are obviously challenging, as a series of longitudinal case studies would be required, to allow assessment of the evolving relationship between the various contracting concerns. Such a series of studies nonetheless offers great potential, as one could address a rich set of questions, such as the following:

- Does the nature of technology transferred and the scope of projects vary over the life of an alliance? How are governance instruments adapted?
- How do investments in transaction-specific assets develop over the course of an alliance? What is the role (if any) of transaction-specific investments in the equilibration of hazards (i.e. exchange of hostages) in the face of appropriability concerns? Can such investments actually reduce contracting hazards in these circumstances?
- Does the use of alliances over internal development increase during periods of rapid technological change (controlling for possible differences in the nature of the transaction)? What types of alliances are favored in these circumstances?

The prospects for empirical study here are rich and exciting. The challenge is to approach these opportunities in a rigorous and incremental manner, maintaining the strictly comparative institutional approach that is a key advantage of the transaction cost framework.

Synthesis with the "resource-based view"

Despite the criticisms raised earlier, "knowledge-based" and related perspectives on the theory of the firm — collectively known as the "resource-based view" — continue to make valuable contributions to our understanding of inter-firm alliances. In contrast to the governance view of the firm adopted in transaction cost economics, the resource-based view conceives of the firm as a collection of "sticky" and hard-to-imitate assets (Conner, 1991; Wernerfelt, 1984). As such, research in this tradition has focused on the processes by which rents can be captured through protection and deployment of idiosyncratic resources (Barney, 1986; Dierickx & Cool, 1989). More recently, attention has also been paid to the dynamic process of change in capabilities underpinning these resources — notably in the literature on "dynamic capabilities" (Teece & Pisano, 1994; Teece, Pisano, & Shuen, 1997).

Although usually maintaining the firm as the unit of analysis, some researchers in the resource-based tradition have discussed the role of inter-firm alliances in the acquisition of new capabilities through organizational learning (e.g., Teece & Pisano, 1994). An extensive literature has also developed, exploring those features of alliances and their participants which facilitate the flow of technological and other know-how among partner firms (Hamel, 1991; Hamel, Doz, & Prahalad, 1989; Inkpen, 1996). In contrast to TCE, where the capabilities of the transacting partners are treated as exogenous, this stream of research within the resource-based view and related fields allows for a closer examination of the characteristics of firms chosen as alliance partners, and for the "micro-structures" of alliance organization. Although empirical obstacles have meant that much of this work has relied on illustrative and case study approaches rather than on statistical evidence, some significant insights have nonetheless emerged.

Consider, for example, the range of circumstances leading to collaboration, and the issue of partner choice. In transaction cost economics, little attention is given to heterogeneity in capabilities of potential alliance partners (with the exception that a "thin" market in the needed assets leads to small-numbers problems and potential contractual hazards). The decision to collaborate, in this view, turns primarily on the nature of the assets to be combined and the resulting contractual hazards. Where assets are particularly idiosyncratic and hazards are consequently severe, the transaction cost logic suggests that organizing the activity within a single firm is preferred — either by acquiring the assets in question, or by developing them in-house. However, as research in the resource-based view stresses, it is precisely such idiosyncratic firm-specific assets that are difficult to imitate (Barney, 1991; Teece, 1986) and that are often not alienable from their organizational context, at least in the short term (Kogut & Zander, 1992). Thus, where pooling of idiosyncratic assets held be different firms is required, one implication of the resource-based view is that inter-firm collaboration may be the only feasible way to achieve the desired outcome *in a timely fashion*. Thus, in circumstances where a rapid response is called for, alliances may emerge even when contractual hazards greatly exceed the "intermediate range" associated with hybrid organizations in the transaction cost framework. Furthermore, research in the resource-based view can provide insight into partner choice decisions related to the particular portfolio of technological or other capabilities required (see, for example, Mowery, Oxley, & Silverman, 1998).

Transaction cost economics can nonetheless offer additional insight by alerting us to the hazards associated with "capabilities combinations" in alliances *and* highlighting ways in which they can be mitigated. This in turn avoids some of the strategic prescriptions emanating from some research in the resource-based view which relies on a myopic or one-sided treatment of alliance behavior. For example, Hamel et al. (1989) suggest that companies will benefit most from alliances by limiting knowledge transfers to partners, limiting the transparency and scope of resources and capabilities contributed, while simultaneously maximizing learning from partners and systematically diffusing new knowledge throughout the organization. While this advice certainly highlights the hazards associated with collaboration, it portrays alliances as essentially a zero-sum competitive game between partner firms, with each trying to maximize knowledge flows in one direction and minimize flows in the other. Unless one of the partners is quite myopic, this strategy is not sustainable beyond the short-term, and is unlikely to lead to significant learning for either partner. The transaction cost logic developed here emphasizes that it is only through the crafting of a governance structure which allows partner firms to commit credibly to work within the intended parameters of an agreement that meaningful cooperation will be supported.

Despite some important progress in research into inter-firm alliances from the perspectives of transaction cost economics *and* the resource-based view of the firm (as well as other disciplines) there remain significant areas of incomplete understanding. This represents a challenge and an opportunity to conduct research on a phenomenon that has both great importance in itself in this age of "alliance capitalism" (Gerlach, 1992) as well as having implications for broader theoretical debates on the theory of the firm. The overall goal of such a research agenda is to systematically analyze why firms enter alliances, with whom, and for what; and how they organize to maximize benefits, contributing to the "continuing search for rent" that is the essence of strategy (Bowman, 1974, p. 47, quoted in Mahoney & Pandian, 1992). Complete answers to these questions require a more fundamental understanding of the nature of learning, as well as of the basic conflicts faced by alliance partners, and the role of governance in managing these conflicts. This is a large undertaking, and will require, at a minimum, the combined power of both the resource-based and transaction cost perspectives, if not an even broader interdisciplinary attack.

Focusing in on the specifics of a medium-term research agenda exploring learning and hazard mitigation issues in alliances, and capitalizing on the complementarities between transaction cost economics and the knowledge- and resource-based views of the firm, I would propose the following questions:

1. *How do firms choose alliance partners?* Work has begun here, combining the focus on capabilities and resources from the resource-based view with issues of reputation and informal governance mechanisms from transaction cost economics, and sociology's emphasis on the "embeddedness" aspects of networks that influence alliance partner choice (e.g., Gulati, 1995b; Mowery et al., in press). As measurement of capabilities and firm-specific resources improves, making more fine-grained empirical assessment feasible, and as our understanding of the interactions of the social and economic features of networks develops, this research should yield interesting new insights into alliance activity.

2. *How do alliance partner capabilities change over time?* How do characteristics of the partner firms' capabilities and know-how, organizational processes, and governance, interact and evolve over the course of an alliance? Work in this area is limited to date. There are several small-scale case studies that provide rich description of knowledge-acquisition processes within alliances, but more limited systematic analysis (Hamel, 1991; Hamel et al., 1989; Inkpen, 1996). In addition, some recent "comparative static" analyses compare partner resources before and after alliance establishment, and infer changes in capabilities from observed differences (Mowery et al., 1996; Nakamura, Shaver, & Yeung, 1996). A useful and logical next step in this research stream would be to conduct careful longitudinal studies examining the evolution of governance structures and organizational processes for managing inter-firm knowledge transfers and learning over the course of an alliance. One would expect, for example, that these structures would change as the balance shifts between transfers of pre-existing knowledge resources among partner firms and the creation of new know-how.

3. *What are the sources and implications of persistent inter-firm heterogeneity in the organization of external economic*

relations? While the transaction cost economics framework has proven successful in explaining the choice of governance structure for individual transactions within a firm (or alliance), there remains a large variance in the overall degree of integration adopted by different firms which resists straightforward explanation (see, for example, Monteverde & Teece, 1982). Recent research suggests that this heterogeneity is a reflection of inter-firm differences in capabilities or expertise in managing different types of economic relationships. For example, there is evidence of considerable differences in the degree to which American and Japanese automobile companies utilize complex alliance forms in their dealings with suppliers. It has been argued that this is in fact an important source of competitive advantage for Japanese automakers (Dyer, 1996; Dyer & Singh, in press). Furthermore, while firms can change the way that they manage external economic relations, this is a complex and path-dependent process as bundles of mutually reinforcing processes or routines must be adopted simultaneously (Dyer, 1997). Understanding the interplay between efforts to realign transactions with appropriate governance structures, and the capabilities necessary to achieve this realignment is another line of inquiry that can benefit from a combined TCE/resource-based view approach. It also offers the potential to enrich each of the theories in the process, providing insight into the details and dynamics of governance mechanisms and the process of changing capabilities and resources.

Of course this list of potential research questions is by no means exhaustive, and there will be new areas of inquiry that open up as we move ahead. If alliance activity continues at the pace of the past decade or so, the demand for information on the best way to structure and manage these alliances will continue to grow. Hopefully, the research reported here, along with work in the tradition from which it springs, will contribute to the understanding of organizational developments as they unfold.

Endnotes

THE MARKET-HIERARCHY CONTINUUM OF HYBRID ORGANIZATIONS

1. Indeed, in later work with Roos (Lorange & Roos, 1992), Lorange backs away from this detailed ordering of forms, and presents a simplified continuum of cooperative ventures, based on the degree of "vertical integration." Going from most to least hierarchical, these are: mergers and acquisitions; joint ownership; joint venture; formal cooperative venture and; informal cooperative venture. The relevant features of the organizational forms in this new continuum are not specified in detail, and it is not clear how the old continuum maps into the new one.

2. Portions of this and the following two chapters draw on Oxley (1997).

3. Opportunism is further defined as the "incomplete or distorted disclosure of information, especially . . . calculated efforts to mislead, distort, disguise, obfuscate or otherwise confuse" (Williamson, 1985, p. 47).

4. Transaction-specific assets are defined as "durable investments that are undertaken in support of particular transactions, the opportunity cost of which investments is much lower in best alternative uses or by alternative users should the original transaction be terminated." (Williamson, 1985, p. 55) The emphasis on asset specificity in the following discussion of the basic TCE model reflects the "mainstream" of work in the field.

5. This is the type of adaptation Hayek (1945) had in mind when he referred to the "marvel" of the market as an adaptive mechanism.

6. Governance costs include the ex ante transaction costs of negotiating and writing contracts as well as ex post costs of haggling, losses associated with the failure to restore positions on the shifting "contract curve," court action and other dispute settlement costs, shirking and other bureaucratic costs (Williamson, 1985, p. 388).

7. Bureaucratic costs include the direct costs of administrative controls, as well as costs related to shirking, "over-managing,"

influence costs and politicization, (March & Simon, 1958; Milgrom & Roberts, 1990; Williamson, 1985)

8. Spiller, P. (1985) also examines site-specificity in vertical mergers, and finds greater support for the asset specificity explanation of mergers than for market-power explanations. In addition, Masten, Meehan, and Snyder (1991) identify a condition akin to site specificity, which they term "temporal specificity," where timely responsiveness by on-site personnel is vital.

9. The effect of such physical asset specificity on make-vs-buy decisions has received significant empirical attention, although often in conjunction with examination of human asset specificity (Masten, 1984; Masten, Meehan, & Snyder, 1989; Monteverdi & Teece, 1982). Lock-in problems associated with physical asset specificity alone may be avoided simply by concentrating the ownership of the assets themselves on the buyer, and putting the business out for bid (Teece, 1981; Williamson, 1985).

10. There appears to be little documentation of an independent effect of such dedicated assets on integration. Instead, the contractual relation may be expanded to allow "hostage exchange" which equilibrates the exposure of the trading parties (Williamson, 1985, p. 96).

11. The costs associated with the loss of a "specific" employee are explained as follows by Nelson and Winter: "[In] some cases the memory of a single organization member may be the sole storage point of knowledge that is both idiosyncratic and of great importance to the organization . . . The loss of an employee with such important idiosyncratic knowledge poses a major threat to the continuity of routine" (p. 115).

12. The use of hostage exchanges to build credible commitments is explained more generally and more completely in Williamson (1985, pp. 163–197). The role of mutual hostage positions in joint ventures is also stressed by Kogut (1988).

13. See Crocker and Reynolds (1993) for a description and transaction cost analysis of various types of compensation schemes used in government procurement contracts, and Williamson (1991) and Joskow (1985, 1988, 1990) for discussion of the price adjustment provisions in long term coal supply contracts.

APPROPRIABILITY HAZARDS AND GOVERNANCE

1. The focus here is primarily on the US. Discussion of international differences in intellectual property protection can be found in Chapter 5.
2. See Benko (1987) for a more complete description of the requirements of the different legal instruments, and rights conferred, and for discussion of the legislation underlying US intellectual property rules.
3. This finding is consistent with earlier studies of industries' dependence on patents (Taylor & Silberston, 1973), and with the findings of Levin et al. (1987) on the relative importance of different methods of appropriating the returns from industrial R&D.
4. Imitation costs are defined to include all costs of developing and introducing the imitative product, including applied research, product specification, pilot plant or prototype construction, investment in plant and equipment, and manufacturing and marketing startup. If there was a patent on the innovations, the cost of investing around it is included.
5. The distinction between product and process should be used with care, however, since an innovation may be seen as a product by the innovator, but may be used in a process role by the customer.

AN EMPIRICAL STUDY OF APPROPRIABILITY HAZARDS IN INTERNATIONAL STRATEGIC ALLIANCES STAGE 1: US-BASED FIRMS

1. "Global" alliances in this context refer to alliances between US-based multinationals that explicitly cover operations in several countries.
2. This characterization does not imply an intertemporal response but, rather, a cross-sectional observation.
3. Studies of international business arrangements have focused primarily on the choice between autonomous investment and joint venturing. For a discussion of inconsistencies in the observed effects of some of these firm level variables on the propensity to invest autonomously, see Gomes-Casseres (1989).

4. There are, of course, differences in the efficacy of patent protection across industries, due to differences in technology, and the ease with which property rights can be specified and enforced (Levin et al., 1987; Mansfield, 1986). This is again related to the issue of "tacitness," as the following quote from the study by Levin et al. suggests:

    The most probable explanation for the robust finding that patents are particularly effective in chemical industries is that comparatively clear standards can be applied to assess a chemical patent's validity and defend against infringement. The uniqueness of a specific molecule is more easily demonstrated than the novelty of, for example, a new component of a complex electrical or mechanical system (p. 798).

    Ideally, one would thus include in the empirical model industry-level measures of the efficacy of formal instruments of intellectual property protection, such as those developed by Levin et al. Unfortunately, incompatibilities between these data and the industry categories used in the CATI database render such an exercise futile, (see Oxley, 1995, for details).

5. Hagedoorn and Duysters (1993, p. 1) describe the shortcomings of the data as follows: " . . . skewness in the distribution of modes of cooperation (i.e. an underestimation of the number of customer-supplier relations and licensing agreements, due to underreporting in published media), . . . some geographic — i.e. Anglo Saxon — bias . . . an underestimation of certain technological fields not belonging to modern core technologies and . . . some over representation of large firms."

6. Because Compustat data is based on firm-level observations, and many of the firms in the CATI database are actually subsidiaries of larger companies, the first step in obtaining this information was to match subsidiaries with their parent companies in the year the alliance was established. This was accomplished using the *Directory of Corporate Affiliations* for the relevant years.

7. This reflects the large proportion of multi-partner alliances with at least one private or non-manufacturing firm for which Compustat data was unavailable.

8. .Other sectors accounting for significant numbers of alliances in the sample are aircraft, automobiles, consumer electronics, defense, electrical equipment, engineering, and instruments.

9. All of the firm-specific information is for the year of establishment of the alliance in question. Firms assets are deflated to 1982 levels based on the capital goods producer price index (U.S. Department of Commerce, 1992).

10. The probit model assumes that the underlying probability distribution is normal. In the common alternative to this model, the logit, the probability distribution is assumed to be logistic. The difference between these cumulative distributions is small, except in the tails, so the results should not be sensitive to the choice between these models, unless there is a large number of observations in the tails (Maddala, 1983). To ensure that this condition was not operable in the samples analyzed here, the models were estimated using both ordered probit and ordered logit. No significant differences in the results were observed, and so only the ordered probit results are reported.

11. Previous studies of franchising arrangements suggest an alternative explanation for the negative coefficient on geographic scope. In several studies, (Brickley & Dark, 1987; Lafontaine, 1992; Minkler, 1990) measures of geographic dispersion, such as distance from monitoring headquarters or number of states in which the chain has outlets, are used as proxies for difficulties in direct monitoring of agents' effort. These variables are found to be negatively related to the probability that an outlet will be company-owned. The inference is that monitoring difficulties increase the need for high-powered incentives, and thus increase the attractiveness of contractual (versus integrated) solutions. However, in the current study focusing on appropriability hazards in alliances, high-powered incentives have perverse effects, as they increase the probability that technology will be put to uncompensated use outside the scope of the agreement. More hierarchical governance modes are thus the expected response to increased difficulties in monitoring.

12. This robustness suggests that the bias in the "public firm sample" does not have a material effect. This is consistent with the logic of the model, since the theory operates at the level of the transaction rather than at the firm level. Therefore, absent systematic differences in transactions tied to characteristics of the firm, sample biases in firm characteristics should be inconsequential.

AN EMPIRICAL STUDY OF APPROPRIABILITY HAZARDS
IN INTERNATIONAL STRATEGIC ALLIANCES
STAGE 2: CROSS-NATIONAL COMPARISONS

1. Portions of this chapter draw on Oxley (in press).
2. The effective duration of patent protection is the length of protection granted from the time of the grant date. In countries where the "official" length of protection granted is counted from the date of application, this must be reduced by the average delay from filing to grant to assess the effective duration of patent protection.
3. While the governance costs associated with equity joint ventures are also likely to rise in these circumstances, they will do so at a lower rate than is expected for contractual arrangements (because of the incentive properties discussed earlier). It is the change in *relative* governance costs of the two modes that will determine the optimal governance arrangement for a particular transaction.
4. Other criticisms and shortcomings of Rapp and Rozek's index include the omitence of enforcement or implementation issues, and the "snapshot" nature of the index, which was compiled for a single year — 1988. Business International Corporation also provides evaluations of protection of industrial property rights, primarily for developing countries. However, this data can support, at best, broad categorical coding of intellectual property protection (see, for example, Chi & Roehl, 1997) and the country coverage is inadequate for the purposes of the current study.
5. This refers to protection against losses arising from compulsory licensing, "working" requirements or revocation of patents.
6. Each of these categories is given a score in the range of 0–1 and the *IPINDEX* is the unweighted sum of the five values. See Park & Ginarte (1997) for a more complete discussion of the measurement of patent provisions and determination of the index, including sensitivity of the index to changes in specification.
7. Another limitation of *IPINDEX* is that the measure is available only quinquennially. Intellectual property protection was actually quite stable over the sample period (1980–89) in most countries, with either no major change or just one or two discrete changes in patent laws and enforcement in some countries. The discrete nature of the changes suggests that interpolation is not

an appropriate way to assess the strength of protection for the interim years. Instead, the 1980 value of *IPINDEX*$_i$ is used for alliances established in 1980–82, the 1985 value for alliances with establishment dates 1983–87 and the 1990 value for those established in 1988–89.

8. For country j, $\text{CULDIST}_j = S_{k=1-4}\{(I_{k,j} - I_{k,us})^2/V_k\}/4$, where $I_{k=1-4}$ are the indices of the four cultural dimensions, V_k is the respective variance, and us indicates the United States.

9. See Shane (1994, pp. 629–630) for a more complete discussion of the use of this measure as a proxy for societal trust.

10. Note that there are significant changes occurring in investment regulations as a result of the TRIMs (Trade Related Investment Measures) agreement, part of the most recent GATT settlement. However, these changes post-date the sample period, and many of the same conditions apply here as in the TRIPs agreement, discussed earlier.

11. Contractor's (1990) second index, measuring restrictions on equity holdings, is not adopted, as the Benchmark Survey documents only equity restrictions affecting the choice between minority- and majority-owned affiliates — not the choice between equity-based joint ventures and contract-based alliances. Furthermore, there are no countries in the sample with an outright ban on foreign equity holdings which would be expected to have a more direct effect on the choice under investigation. On the other hand, in countries where performance requirements are imposed on majority-owned affiliates these may be extended to all equity joint ventures, potentially increasing the cost of this governance mode relative to a contractual arrangement with a local firm. Thus the performance requirement measure is relevant to this study.

12. Even for the choice between joint ventures and wholly-owned subsidiaries, the impact of political risk is multifaceted and complex (see Henisz, 1998).

13. The validity of this measure of political and economic risk is supported by a study demonstrating that the index is replicable using objective host country economic and political data (Cosset & Roy, 1991).

14. For example, Contractor (1990) finds support for the argument that increased market size increases host government bargaining power, which allows them to enforce their preference for

joint ventures with local producers (so increasing the observed incidence of joint ventures relative to wholly-owned subsidiaries). Davidson and McFetridge (1984) argue for the reverse effect (with foreign direct investment being encouraged, relative to market modes of entry, when market size is large). However, they find no relationship between market size and observed patterns of foreign entry governance mode.

15.   These results are from a model which included, as independent variables, only the transaction level variables from the Stage 1 analysis and *IPINDEX* (the appropriability measure). However, adding additional explanatory variables did not improve the predictive power of the model. Coefficient estimates in the more "complete" model were, nonetheless, consistent with those reported below for the binomial logit model.

16.   Very similar results were obtained from estimation of a binomial probit model. The logit was adopted to allow straightforward calculation of the "economic significance" of the independent variables (see below).

17.   The models estimated below are without these dummies added, but all of the results were replicated without significant changes with area and year dummies added, as well as with a single time trend variable with values from 1 for alliances established in 1980 to 10 for alliances established in 1989.

References

Agarwal, S. & Ramaswami, S. (1992). "Choice of foreign market entry mode: Impact of ownership, location and internalization factors". *Journal of International Business Studies*, 23 (First Quarter), 1–27.

Alchian, A. A. & Demsetz, H. (1972). "Production, information costs and economic organization". *American Economic Review*, 62, 777–795.

Amburgey, T. L. & Miner, A. S. (1992). "Strategic momentum: The effects of repetitive, positional and contextual momentum on merger activity". *Strategic Management Journal*, 13, 335–348.

Anderson, E. (1985). "The salesperson as outside agent or employee: A transaction cost analysis". *Marketing Science*, 4, 234–54.

Anderson, E. & Schmittlein, D. C. (1984). "Integration of the sales force: An empirical examination". *Rand Journal of Economics*, 15(3), 385–95.

Arrow, K. J. (1962). "Economic welfare and the allocation of resources of invention", in National Bureau of Economics Research (Ed.), *The rate and direction of inventive activity: Economic and social factors*, 609–25. Princeton, NJ: Princeton University Press.

Arrow, K. J. (1971). *Essays in the theory of risk-bearing.* Chicago: Markham.

Arrow, K. J. (1973). *Information and economic behavior.* Stockholm: Federation of Swedish Industries.

Balakrishnan, S. & Koza, M. P. (1993). "Information assymmetry, adverse selection and joint ventures". *Journal of Economic Behavior and Organization*, 20, 99–117.

Barney, J. B. (1986). "Strategic factor markets: Expectations, luck and business strategy". *Management Science*, 32 (10), 1231–1241.

Barro, R. & Lee, J. (1993). *International comparisons of educational attainment.* Cambridge, MA: National Bureau of Economic Research.

Behrman, J. & Wallender, H. (1976). *Transfers of manufacturing technology within multinational enterprises.* Cambridge, MA: Ballinger.

Benko, R. P. (1987). *Protecting intellectual property rights: Issues and controversies.* Washington D.C.: American Enterprise Institute for Public Policy Research.

Bowman, E. H. (1974). "Epistemology, corporate strategy and academe". *Sloan Management Review*, 15 (2), 35–50.

Brickley, J. & Dark, F. (1987). "The choice of organizational form: The case of franchising". *Journal of Financial Economics*, 18, 401–420.

Brodley, J. (1982). "Joint ventures and antitrust policy". *Harvard Law Review*, 1523–90.

Chandler, A. D. (1977). *The visible hand: The managerial revolution in american business*. Cambridge, MA: Belknap/Harvard University Press.

Chang, H. (1991). *Patent scope, antitrust policy and cumulative innovation*. Discussion Paper # 96, Harvard Law School.

Chaudhry, P. E. & Walsh, M. G. (1995). "Intellectual property rights: Changing levels of protection under GATT, NAFTA and the EU". *Columbia Journal of World Business*, 30 (Summer), 80–91.

Chi, T. & Roehl, T. W. (1997). "The structuring of interfirm exchanges in business know-how: Evidence from international collaborative ventures". *Managerial and Decision Economics*, 18, 279–294.

Coase, R. H. (1937). "The nature of the firm". *Economica*, 4, 386–405.

Cohen, W. M. & Levinthal, D. A. (1990). "Absorptive capacity: A new perspective on learning and innovation". *Administrative Science Quarterly*, 35, 569–596.

Conner, K. R. (1991). "A historical comparison of resource-based theory and five schools of thought within industrial organization economics: Do we have a new theory of the firm?" *Journal of Management*, 17, 121–154.

Conner, K. R. & Prahalad, C. K. (1996). "A resource-based theory of the firm: Knowledge versus opportunism". *Organization Science*, 7 (5), 477–501.

Contractor, F. (1990). "Ownership patterns of U.S. joint ventures abroad and the liberalization of foreign government regulations in the 1980s: Evidence from the benchmark surveys". *Journal of International Business Studies*, 21 (First Quarter), 55–73.

Contractor, F. J. & Lorange, P. (1988). "Why should firms cooperate? The strategy and economics basis for cooperative ventures", in F. J. Contractor & P. Lorange (Eds.), *Cooperative strategies in international business*, 3–28. Lexington, MA: Lexington Books.

Cosset, J. C. & Roy, J. (1991). "The determinants of country risk ratings", *Journal of International Business Studies*, 22 (1), 135–142.

Crocker, K. J. & Reynolds, K. J. (1993). "The efficiency of incomplete contracts: An empirical analysis of air force engine procurement". *Rand Journal of Economics*, 24 (1), 126–46.

Davidson, W. H. & McFetridge, D. G. (1984). "International technology transactions and the theory of the firm". *Journal of Industrial Economics*, 32 (3), 253–264.

Davidson, W. H. & McFetridge, D. G. (1985). "Key characteristics in the choice of international technology transfer mode". *Journal of International Business Studies*, 16 (Summer), 5–21.

Davis, L. E. & North, D. C. (1971). *Institutional change and american economic growth*. Cambridge, U.K.: Cambridge University Press.

Dierickx, I. & Cool, K. (1989). "Asset stock accumulation and sustainability of competitive advantage". *Management Science*, 35 (12), 1504–1514.

Directory of Corporate Affiliations (1980–89). Skokie, IL: National Register Publishing Co.

Duysters, G. & Hagedoorn, J. (1996). "Internationalization of corporate technology through strategic partnering: An empirical investigation". *Research Policy*, 25, 1–12.

Dyer, J. H. (1996). "Specialized supplier networks as a source of competitive advantage: Evidence from the auto industry". *Strategic Management Journal*, 17 (4), 271–292.

Dyer, J. H. (1997). *Improving performance by transforming arms-length relationships to supplier partnerships: the Chrysler case*. Unpublished manuscript, The Wharton School, University of Pennsylvania.

Dyer, J. H. & Singh, H. (in press). "The relational view: Relational rents and sources of interorganizational competitive advantage". *The Academy of Management Review*.

Freeman, C. (1982). *The economics of industrial innovation* (2nd ed.). London: Francis Pinter.

Geringer, J. M. & Hebert, L. (1989). "The importance of control in international joint ventures". *Journal of International Business Studies*, 20 (Summer), 235–254.

Gerlach, M. L. (1992). *Alliance capitalism*. Berkeley: University of California Press.

Gilbert, R. & Shapiro, C. (1990). "Optimal patent length and breadth". *RAND Journal of Economics*, 21, 106–112.

Gomes-Casseres, B. (1989). "Ownership structures of foreign subsidiaries: Theory and evidence". *Journal of Economic Behavior and Organization*, 11, 1–25.

Gomes-Casseres, B. (1990). "Firm ownership preferences and host government restrictions: An integrated approach". *Journal of International Business Studies*, 21 (First Quarter), 1–22.

Gulati, R. (1995a). "Does familiarity breed trust? the implications of repeated ties for contractual choice in alliances". *The Academy of Management Journal*, 38 (1), 85–112.

Gulati, R. (1995b). "Social structure and alliance formation patterns: A longitudinal analysis". *Administrative Science Quarterly*, 40, 619–652.

Hagedoorn, J. (1993). "Understanding the Rationale of Strategic Technology Partnering: Interorganizational Modes of Cooperation and Sectoral Differences". *Strategic Management Journal*, 14, 371–385.

Hagedoorn, J. & Duysters, G. (1993). The Cooperative Agreements and Technology Indicators (CATI) information system. Unpublished manuscript, MERIT, Limbourg, The Netherlands.

Hamel, G. (1991). "Competition for competence and inter-partner learning within international strategic alliances". *Strategic Management Journal*, 12 (S1), 83–103.

Hamel, G. Doz, Y. & Prahalad, C. K. (1989). "Collaborate With Your Competitors – And Win". *Harvard Business Review* (January–February), 133–39.

Harrigan, K. R. (1986). *Managing for joint venture success*. Lexington, MA: Lexington Books.

Harrigan, K. R. (1988). "Strategic alliances and partner asymmetries", in F. J. Contractor & P. Lorange (Eds.), *Cooperative Strategies in International Business*, 205–226. Lexington, MA: Lexington Books.

Hayek, F. (1945). "The use of knowledge in society". *American Economic Review*, 35 (September), 519–30.

Henisz, W. J. (1998). *The institutional environment for international investment: Safeguarding against state sector opportunism and opportunistic use of the state*, Ph.D. dissertation, Haas School of Business, University of California at Berkeley.

Hennart, J.-F. (1988a). "Upstream vertical integration in the aluminum and tin industries". *Journal of Economic Behavior and Organization*, 9, 281–99.

Hennart, J.-F. (1988b). "A Transaction costs theory of equity joint ventures". *Strategic Management Journal*, 9, 361–374.

Hennart, J.-F. (1991). "The transaction costs theory of joint ventures: An empirical study of japanese subsidiaries in the U.S." *Management Science*, 37 (4), 483–497.

Hergert, M. & Morris, D. (1988). "Trends in international collaborative agreements", in F. Contractor & P. Lorange (Eds.), *Cooperative Strategies in International Business*, 99–110. Lexington, MA: Lexington Books.

Hill, C., Hwang, P. & Kim, W. C. (1990). "An eclectic theory of the choice of international entry mode". *Strategic Management Journal*, 11, 117–28.

Hladik, K. (1985). *International joint ventures: An economic analysis of U.S.-foreign business partnerships*. Lexington, MA: Lexington Books.

Hofstede, G. H. (1980). *Culture's consequences: International differences in work-related values*. Beverly Hills, CA: Sage Publications.

Inkpen, A. C. (1996). "Creating knowledge through collaboration". *California Management Review*, 39 (1), 123–140.

John, G. & Weitz, B. A. (1988). "Forward integration into distribution: An empirical test of transaction cost analysis". *Journal of Law, Economics and Organization*, 4, 337–55.

Joskow, P. L. (1985). "Vertical integration and long-term contracts: The case of coal-burning electrical generating plants". *Journal of Law, Economics and Organization*, 1, 33–88.

Joskow, P. L. (1988). "Price adjustments in long-term contracts: The case of coal". *Journal of Law and Economics*, 31, 47–83.

Joskow, P. L. (1990). "The performance of long-term contracts: further evidence from the coal markets". *Rand Journal of Economics*, 21 (2), 251–74.

Killing, J. P. (1983). *Strategies for joint venture success*. London, UK: Croom Helm.

Kim, W. C. & Hwang, P. (1992). "Global strategy and multinationals' entry mode choice". *Journal of International Business*, 23, (First Quarter), 29–53.

Klemperer, P. (1990). "How broad should the scope of patent protection be?". *RAND Journal of Economics*, 21(1), 113–130.

Kobrin, S. J. (1976). "The environmental determinants of foreign direct investment: An ex post empirical analysis". *Journal of International Business Studies*, 7, 29–42.

Kogut, B. (1988). "Joint ventures: Theoretical and empirical perspectives". *Strategic Management Journal*, 9, 319–332.

Kogut, B. (1989). "The stability of joint ventures: Reciprocity and competitive rivalry". *The Journal of Industrial Economics*, 38 (2), 183–198.

Kogut, B. & Chang, S. J. (1991). "Technological capabilities and Japanese foreign direct investment in the United States". *The Review of Economics and Statistics*, 401–413.

Kogut, B. & Singh, H. (1988). "The effect of national culture on the choice of entry mode". *Journal of International Business Studies* (Fall), 411–432.

Kogut, B. & Zander, U. (1992). "Knowledge of the firm, combinative capabilities and the replication of technology". *Organization Science*, 3, 383–397.

Kogut, B. & Zander, U. (1993). Knowledge of the firm and the evolutionary theory of the multinational corporation. *Journal of International Business Studies*, 24(4), 625–45.

Kogut, B. & Zander, U. (1996). "What firms do? Coordination, identity and learning". *Organization Science*, 7(5), 502–518.

Kondo, E. K. (1994). *Patent laws and foreign direct investment: An empirical investigation.* Ph.D. dissertation, Harvard University.

Lafontaine, F. (1992). "Agency theory and franchising: Some empirical results". *Rand Journal of Economics*, 23, 263–283.

Lessard, D. R. (1995). "International business as a scholarly domain". *Academy of International Business Newsletter*, 1 (1), 3.

Levin, R. Klevorick, A., Nelson, R. & Winter, S. (1987). "Appropriating the returns from industrial research and development". *Brookings Papers on Economic Activity*, 3, 783–820.

Llewellyn, K. (1931). "What price contract? An essay in perspective". *Yale Law Journal*, 40, 701–751.

Lorange, P. & Roos, J. (1992). *Strategic alliances: Formation, implementation and evolution.* Cambridge, MA: Blackwell.

Macneil, I. R. (1978). "Contracts: Adjustments of long-term economic relations under classical, neoclassical and relational contract law". *Northwestern University Law Review*, 72, 854–906.

Maddala, G. S. (1983). *Limited-dependent and qualitative variables in econometrics.* New York: Cambridge University Press.

Mahoney, J. T. & Pandian, J. R. (1992). "The resource-based view within the conversation of strategic management". *Strategic Management Journal*, 13, 363–380.

Mansfield, E. (1985). "How rapidly does new industrial technology leak out?" *The Journal of Industrial Economics*, 34 (2), 217–223.

Mansfield, E. (1986). "Patents and innovation: An empirical study". *Management Science*, 32 (2), 173–181.

Mansfield, E. (1993). "Unauthorized use of intellectual property: Effects on investment, technology transfer, and innovation", in M. Wallerstein, M. E. Mogee & R. A. Schoen (Eds.), *Global dimensions of intellectual property rights in science and technology*, 107–45. Washington D.C.: National Academy Press.

Mansfield, E. (1994). *Intellectual property protection, foreign direct investment and technology transfer.* International Finance Corporation Discussion Paper, 19, The World Bank.

Mansfield, E. Schwartz, M. & Wagner, S. (1981). "Imitation costs and patents: An empirical study". *The Economic Journal*, 91 (December), 907–918.

March, J. G. & Simon, H. A. (1958). *Organizations.* New York: John Wiley and Sons.

Masten, S. E. (1984). "The organization of production: Evidence from the aerospace industry". *Journal of Law and Economics*, 27, 403–17.

Masten, S. Meehan, J. & Snyder, E. (1991). "The costs of organization". *Journal of Law, Economics and Organization*, 7 (1), 1–25.

Masten, S. E. Meehan, J. W. & Snyder, E. A. (1989). "Vertical integration in the U.S. auto industry: A note on the influence of specific assets". *Journal of Economic Behavior and Organization*, 12, 265–73.

Merges, R. P. & Nelson, R. R. (1992). "Market structure and technical advance: The role of patent scope decisions", in T. Jorde & D. Teece (Eds.), *Antitrust, innovation and competitiveness* 185–232, New York: Oxford University Press.

Milgrom, P. A. & Roberts, J. (1990). "Bargaining costs, influence costs, and the organization of economic activity", in J. E. Alt & K. A. Shepsle (Eds.), *Perspectives on positive political economy* 57–89. Cambridge, U.K.: Cambridge University Press.

Miller, D. & Friesen, P. H. (1980). "Momentum and revolution in organizational adaptation". *Academy of Management Journal*, 23 (4), 591–614.

Minkler, A. (1990). "An empirical analysis of a firm's decision to franchise". *Economics Letters*, 34, 77–82.

Mogee, M. E. (1989). *International trade in chemicals: Intellectual property problems and issues.* Brussels: Organization for Economic Cooperation and Development.

Monteverdi, K. & Teece, D. J. (1982). "Supplier switching costs and vertical integration in the automobile industry". *Bell Journal of Economics*, 13, 206–13.

Mowery, D. C. (1989). "Collaborative ventures between U.S. and foreign manufacturers". *Research Policy*, 18, 19–32.

Mowery, D. C. & Oxley, J. E. (1995). "Inward technology transfer and competitiveness: The role of national innovation systems". *Cambridge Journal of Economics*, 19 (1), 67–94.

Mowery, D. C. Oxley, J. E. & Silverman, B. S. (1996). "Learning in interfirm alliances". *Strategic Management Journal*, 17 (S2), 77–91.

Mowery, D. C. Oxley, J. E. and Silverman, B. S. (1998). "Technological overlap and interfirm cooperation: Implications for the resource-based view of the firm". *Research Policy*, 27, 507–523.

Mowery, D. C. & Rosenberg, N. (1989). *Technology and the pursuit of economic growth*. Cambridge, U.K.: Cambridge University Press.

Nakamura, M. Shaver, J. M. and Yeung, B. (1996). "An empirical investigation of joint venture dynamics: Evidence from U.S.-Japan joint ventures". *International Journal of Industrial Organization*, 14, 521–541.

Nelson, R. R. (1990). *What is public and what is private about technology?* CCC Working Paper, 90–9, University of California at Berkeley

Nelson, R. R. & Winter, S. G. (1982). *An Evolutionary theory of economic change*. Cambridge, MA: Harvard University Press.

Osborn, R. N. & Baughn, C. C. (1990). "Forms of interorganizational governance for multinational alliances". *Academy of Management Journal*, 33 (3), 503–519.

Oxley, J. E. (1995). *International hybrids: A transaction cost treatment and empirical study*. PhD. dissertation, Haas School of Business, University of California at Berkeley.

Oxley, J. E. (1997). "Appropriability hazards and governance in international strategic alliances: A transaction cost approach". *Journal of Law, Economics and Organization* 13 (2), 387–409.

Oxley, J. E. (in press). "Institutional environment and the mechanisms of governance: The impact of intellectual property protection on the structure of inter-firm alliances". *Journal of Economic Behavior and Organization*.

Park, W. G. & Ginarte, J. C. (1997). "Determinants of patent rights: A cross-national study". *Research Policy*, 26 (3), 283–301.

Pisano, G. (1989). "Using equity participation to support exchange: Evidence from the biotechnology industry". *Journal of Law, Economics and Organization*, V (1), 109–26.

Pisano, G. Russo, M. & Teece, D. (1988). "Joint ventures and collaborative arrangements in the telecommunications equipment industry", in D. Mowery (Ed.), *International Collaborative Ventures in US Manufacturing* 23–70. Cambridge, MA: Ballinger.

Porter, M. E. & Fuller, M. B. (1986). "Coalitions and global strategy", in M. E. Porter (Ed.), *Competition in Global Industries.* Boston: Harvard Business School Press.

Rapp, R. & Rozek, R. (1990). "Benefits and costs of intellectual property protection in developing countries". *Journal of World Trade,* 24 (2), 75–102.

Robinson, R. (1988). *The international transfer of technology: theory, issues and practice.* Cambridge, MA: Ballinger.

Root, F. R. & Ahmed, A. A. (1978). "The influence of policy instruments on manufacturing direct foreign investment in developing countries". *Journal of International Business Studies,* 9 (3), 81–93.

Schaan, J. L. (1983). *Parent control and joint venture success: The case of Mexico.* Ph.D. dissertation, University of Western Ontario.

Scherer, F. (1992). *International high-technology competition.* Cambridge, MA: Harvard University Press.

Scotchmer, S. (1991). "Standing on the shoulders of giants: Cumulative research and the patent law". *Journal of Economic Perspectives,* 5 (1), 29–41.

Shane, S. (1994). "The effect of national culture on the choice between licensing and direct foreign investment". *Strategic Management Journal,* 15, 627–642.

Shuen, A. (1994). *Technology sourcing and learning strategies in the semiconductor industry.* PhD. Dissertation, Haas School of Business, University of California at Berkeley.

Simon (1961). *Administrative behavior* (2 ed.). New York: Macmillan.

Spiller, P. (1985). "On vertical mergers". *Journal of Law, Economics and Organization,* 1 (2), 285–312.

Stuckey, J. (1983). *Vertical integration and joint ventures in the aluminum industry.* Cambridge, MA: Harvard University Press.

Summers, R. & Heston, H. (1991). "The Penn world table (mark 5): An expanded set of international comparisons, 1950–1988". *Quarterly Journal of Economics,* 106 (2), 327–368.

Taylor, C. & Silberston, Z. (1973). *The economic impact of the patent system.* Cambridge: Cambridge University Press.

Teece, D. J. (1977). "Technology transfer by multinational firms: The resource costs of transfering technological know-how". *The Economic Journal,* 87 (June), 242–61.

Teece, D. J. (1981). "The market for know-how and the efficient international transfer of technology". *Annals of the American Academy of Political and Social Science*, 458, 81–96.

Teece, D. J. (1985). "Multinational enterprise, internal governance and industrial organization". *American Economic Review*, 75, 233–238.

Teece, D. J. (1986). "Profiting from technological innovation: Implications for integration, collaboration, licensing and public policy". *Research Policy*, 15, 285–305.

Teece, D. J. & Pisano, G. (1994). "The dynamic capabilities of firms: An introduction". *Industrial and Corporate Change*, 3, 537–556.

Teece, D. J. Pisano, G. & Shuen, A. (1997). "Dynamic capabilities and strategic management". *Strategic Management Journal*, 18 (7), 509–533.

U.S. Department of Commerce (1985). *U.S. direct investment abroad, 1982: The benchmark survey.* Washington, D.C.: Author.

U.S. Department of Commerce (1992). *Business statistics, 1963–91.* Washington, D.C.: Author.

U.S. International Trade Commission (1988). *Foreign protection of intellectual property rights and the effect on U.S. industry and trade.* Washington, D.C.: Author.

U.S. General Accounting Office (1993). *Intellectual property rights: U.S. companies' patent experiences in Japan.* Washington, D.C.: Author.

Wernerfelt, B. (1984). "A resource-based view of the firm". *Strategic Management Journal*, 5 (2), 171–170.

Williamson, O. E. (1985). *The economic institutions of capitalism.* New York: The Free Press.

Williamson, O. E. (1991). "Comparative economic organization - The analysis of discrete structural alternatives". *Administrative Science Quarterly*, 36 (4), 269–296.

Williamson, O. E. (1992). "Markets, hierarchies, and the modern corporation. An unfolding perspective". *Journal of Economic Behavior and Organization*, 17 (May), 335–352.

Williamson, O. E. (1996). *The mechanisms of governance.* New York: Oxford University Press.

Williamson, O. E. & Masten, S. (1995). *Transaction cost economics.* Aldershot, UK: Edward Elgar.

Zajac, E. J. and Olsen, C. P. (1993). "From transaction cost to transaction value analysis: Implications for the study of interorganizational strategies". *Journal of Management Studies*, 30(1), 131–145.

Index

For Product Safety Concerns and Information please contact our EU
representative GPSR@taylorandfrancis.com Taylor & Francis Verlag GmbH,
Kaufingerstraße 24, 80331 München, Germany

Printed and bound by CPI Group (UK) Ltd, Croydon, CR0 4YY
12/05/2025
01867598-0003